Addressing Special Education and Disability in the Curriculum... Music

The SEND Code of Practice (2015) has reinforced the requirement that *all* teachers must meet the needs of *all* learners. This topical book provides practical, tried and tested strategies and resources that will support teachers in making music lessons accessible and exciting for all pupils, including those with special needs. The authors draw on a wealth of experience to share their understanding of special educational needs and disabilities and show how the music teacher can reduce or remove any barriers to learning.

Offering strategies that are specific to the context of music teaching, this book will enable teachers to:

- ensure all pupils are able to enjoy and appreciate music;
- find the appropriate musical instruments to suit the individual learner;
- develop approaches for teaching composition in mixed ability classrooms;
- provide opportunities for different types of performance;
- adapt content, approaches and resources for pupils with a wide range of learning needs.

An invaluable tool for continuing professional development, this text will be essential for teachers (and their teaching assistants) seeking guidance specific to teaching music to all pupils, regardless of their individual needs. This book will also be of interest to SENCOs, senior management teams and ITT providers.

In addition to free online resources, a range of appendices provides music teachers with lesson case studies, behaviour plans and guidance on behaviour management and effective teaching. This is an essential tool for music teachers and teaching assistants, and will help to deliver successful inclusive lessons for all pupils.

Victoria Jaquiss specialises in teaching music to children with challenging behaviour, and also works teaching steelpans.

Diane Paterson is a team leader for teaching music to children with learning difficulties and also those with sensory and/or physical impairments.

Addressing Special Educational Needs and Disability in the Curriculum

Series editor: Linda Evans

Children and young people with a diverse range of special educational needs and disabilities (SEND) are expected to access the full curriculum. Crucially, the current professional standards make it clear that *every* teacher must take responsibility for *all* pupils in their classes. Titles in this fully revised and updated series will be essential for teachers seeking subject-specific guidance on meeting their pupils' individual needs. In line with recent curriculum changes, the new Code of Practice for SEN and other pedagogical developments, these titles provide clear, practical strategies and resources that have proved to be effective and successful in their particular subject area. Written by practitioners, they can be used by departmental teams and in 'whole-school' training sessions as professional development resources. With free Web-based online resources also available to complement the books, these resources will be an asset to any teaching professional helping to develop policy and provision for learners with SEND.

The new national curriculum content will prove challenging for many learners, and teachers of children in Y5 and Y6 will also find the books a valuable resource.

Titles in this series include:

Addressing Special Educational Needs and Disability in the Curriculum: Modern Foreign Languages
John Connor

Addressing Special Educational Needs and Disability in the Curriculum: Music
Victoria Jaquiss and Diane Paterson

Addressing Special Educational Needs and Disability in the Curriculum: PE and Sport
Crispin Andrews

Addressing Special Educational Needs and Disability in the Curriculum: Science
Marion Frankland

Addressing Special Educational Needs and Disability in the Curriculum: Design and Technology
Louise T. Davies

Addressing Special Educational Needs and Disability in the Curriculum: History
Ian Luff and Richard Harris

Addressing Special Educational Needs and Disability in the Curriculum: Religious Education
Dilwyn Hunt

Addressing Special Educational Needs and Disability in the Curriculum: Geography
Graeme Eyre

Addressing Special Educational Needs and Disability in the Curriculum: Art
Gill Curry and Kim Earle

Addressing Special Educational Needs and Disability in the Curriculum: English
Tim Hurst

Addressing Special Educational Needs and Disability in the Curriculum: Maths
Max Wallace

Addressing Special Educational Needs and Disability in the Curriculum: Music

Second edition

Victoria Jaquiss and Diane Paterson

Routledge
Taylor & Francis Group

LONDON AND NEW YORK

Second edition published 2017
by Routledge
2 Park Square, Milton Park, Abingdon, Oxon OX14 4RN

and by Routledge
711 Third Avenue, New York, NY 10017

Routledge is an imprint of the Taylor & Francis Group, an informa business

First edition published 2005 by David Fulton Publishers as *Meeting SEN in the Curriculum: Music*

British Library Cataloguing-in-Publication Data
A catalogue record for this book is available from the British Library

Library of Congress Cataloging-in-Publication Data
Names: Jaquiss, Victoria. | Paterson, Diane.
Title: Addressing special educational needs and disability in the curriculum : music / Victoria Jaquiss and Diane Paterson.
Description: New York : Routledge, 2017. | Includes bibliographical references.
Identifiers: LCCN 2016049725| ISBN 9781138231832 (hardback) | ISBN 9781138231849 (pbk.) | ISBN 9781315314099 (ebook)
Subjects: LCSH: Children with disabilities—Education. | School music—Instruction and study. | Emotional problems of children.
Classification: LCC LC4025 .J37 2017 | DDC 371.9—dc23
LC record available at https://lccn.loc.gov/2016049725

ISBN: 978-1-138-23183-2 (hbk)
ISBN: 978-1-138-23184-9 (pbk)
ISBN: 978-1-315-31409-9 (ebk)

Typeset in Helvetica
by Keystroke, Neville Lodge, Tettenhall, Wolverhampton

Visit the eResources: www.routledge.com/9781138231849

Contents

Appendices

Series authors

The authors

Victoria Jaquiss trained as a teacher of English and drama and held posts of English teacher and head of PSE, music and expressive arts at Foxwood School. She became a recognised authority on behaviour management and inclusion with children in challenging circumstances. The second half of her career has involved working for the Leeds Music Service/ArtForms as Steel Pan Development Officer and deputy inclusion manager/teacher. She was awarded the fellowship of the Royal Society of Arts in 2002.

Diane Paterson began teaching as a mainstream secondary music teacher. She went on to study how music technology could enable people with severe physical difficulties to make their own music, joining the Drake Music project in Yorkshire and becoming its regional leader. She then became inclusion manager/teacher at Leeds Music Service/ArtForms, working with children with additional needs. As secretary of YAMSEN: SpeciallyMusic, she now runs specialist regional workshops, music days and concerts for students with special/additional needs and their carers.

A dedicated team of SEN specialists and subject specialists have contributed to this series.

Series editor

Linda Evans was commissioning editor for the original books in this series and has co-ordinated the updating process for these new editions. She has taught children of all ages over the years and posts have included those of SENCO, LA adviser, Ofsted inspector and HE tutor/lecturer. She was awarded a PhD in 2000, following research on improving educational outcomes for children (primary and secondary).

Since then, Linda has been commissioning editor for David Fulton Publishing (SEN) as well as editor of a number of educational journals and newsletters: she has also written books, practical classroom resources, Master's course materials and school improvement guidance. She maintains her contact with school practitioners through her work as a part-time ITT tutor and educational consultant.

SEND specialist

Sue Briggs has been supporting the education and inclusion of children with special educational needs and disabilities, and their parents, for over 20 years, variously as teacher, Oftsed inspector, specialist member of the SEN and Disability Tribunal, school improvement partner, consultant and adviser. She holds a Master's degree in education, a first class BEd and a diploma in special education (DPSE distinction). Sue was a national lead for the Achievement for All programme (2011–2013) and a regional adviser for the Early Support Programme for the Council for Disabled Children (2014–2015) and is currently an independent education and leadership consultant.

Sue is the author of several specialist books and publications, including *Meeting SEND in Primary Classrooms* and *Meeting SEND in Secondary Classrooms* (Routledge, 2015).

Subject specialists

Art

Gill Curry was Head of Art in a secondary school in Wirral for 20 years and Advisory Teacher for Art and Gifted and Talented Strand Coordinator. She has an MA in Print from the University of Chester and an MA in Women's Studies from the University of Liverpool. She is a practising artist specialising in print and exhibits nationally and internationally, running courses regularly in schools and print studios.

Kim Earle is Vice Principal at Birkenhead High School Academy for Girls on the Wirral. She has previously been a Head of Art and Head of Creative Arts, securing Artsmark Gold in all the establishments in which she has worked. Kim was also formerly Able Pupils and Arts Consultant in St Helens, working across special schools and mainstream schools with teaching and support staff on art policy and practice. She still teaches art in a mixed ability setting in her current school and works closely with local schools and outside organisations to address barriers to learning.

Design and technology

Louise T. Davies is founder of the Food Teachers Centre, offering advice and guidance to the DfE and other organisations based on her years of experience as a teacher and teacher trainer, and her role in curriculum development at QCA and the Royal College of Art. She led innovation at the Design and Technology Association, providing expertise for a range of curriculum and CPD programmes and specialist advice on teaching standards and best practice, including meeting special educational needs. Most recently, she has worked as Lead Consultant for the School Food Champions programme (2013–16) and as an adviser to the DfE on the new GCSE Food Preparation and Nutrition.

English

Tim Hurst began his career as an English teacher at the Willian School in Hertfordshire, becoming Second in English before deciding that his future lay in SEND. He studied for an Advanced Diploma in Special Educational Needs and has been a SEN co-ordinator in five schools in Hertfordshire, Essex and Suffolk. Tim has always been committed to the concept of inclusion and is particularly interested in reading development, which he passionately believes in as a whole school responsibility.

Geography

Graeme Eyre has considerable experience of teaching and leading geography in secondary schools in a range of different contexts, and is currently Assistant Principal for Intervention at an academy in inner London. Graeme is a consultant to the Geographical Association and a Fellow of the Royal Geographical Society. He has also delivered training and CPD for teachers at all levels. He holds a BA in Geography, a PGCE in Secondary Geography and an MA in Geography Education.

History

Ian Luff retired as Deputy Headteacher of Kesgrave High School in 2013 after a 32-year career during which he had been Head of History in four comprehensive schools and an Advisory Teacher with the London Borough of Barking and Dagenham. He is an Honorary Fellow of the Historical Association and currently works as an Associate Tutor on the PGCE history course at the University of East Anglia and as a consultant in history education.

Richard Harris has been teaching since 1989. He has taught in three comprehensive schools, as history teacher, Head of Department and Head of Faculty. He has also worked as teacher consultant for secondary history in West Berkshire. Since 2001 he has been involved in history initial teacher education, firstly at the University of Southampton and more recently at the University of Reading. He has also worked extensively with the Historical Association and Council of Europe in the areas of history education and teacher training, and has been made an Honorary Fellow of the Historical Association. He is currently Associate Professor in history education and Director of Teaching and Learning at the Institute of Education, University of Reading.

Maths

Max Wallace has nine years' experience of teaching children with special educational needs. He currently works as an Advanced Skills Teacher at an inclusive mainstream secondary school. Appointed as a specialist Leader in Education for Mathematics, Max mentors and coaches teachers in a wide network of schools. He has previously worked as a Head of Year and was responsible for the continuing professional development of colleagues. He has a doctorate in mathematics from Cardiff University.

Languages

John Connor is a former head of faculty, local authority adviser and senior examiner. He has also served as an Ofsted team inspector for modern languages and special educational needs in mainstream settings. John was also an assessor on the Advanced Skills Teacher programme for the DfE. He is currently working as a trainer, author and consultant, and has directed teaching and learning quality audits across England, the Channel Islands, Europe, the Middle East and the Far East. He is also a governor of a local primary school.

PE and sport

Crispin Andrews is a qualified teacher and sports coach and has worked extensively in Buckinghamshire schools, coaching cricket and football and developing opportunities for girls in these two sports. He is currently a sports journalist, writing extensively for a wide range of educational journals, including *Special Children* and the *Times Educational Supplement* and other publications such as *Cricket World*.

Religious education

Dilwyn Hunt taught RE for 18 years, before becoming an adviser first in Birmingham and then in Dudley. He currently works as an independent RE adviser supporting local authorities, SACREs and schools. He is also in demand across the country as a speaker on all aspects of teaching RE in both mainstream and special settings. He is the author of numerous popular classroom resources and books and currently serves as the executive assistant for the Association of RE Inspectors, Advisers and Consultants.

Science

Marion Frankland, CSciTeach, has been teaching for 16 years and was an Advanced Skills Teacher of Science. She has extensive experience of teaching science at all levels in both mainstream and special schools and has worked as a SENCO in a special school, gaining her qualification alongside her teaching commitments.

A few words from the series editor

The original version of this book formed part of the 'Meeting SEN in the Curriculum' series which was published ten years ago to much acclaim. The series won a BERA (British Educational Resources Award) and has been widely used by ITT providers, their students and trainees, curriculum and SEN advisers, department heads and teachers of all levels of experience. It has proven to be highly successful in helping to develop policy and provision for learners with Special Educational Needs or Disabilities.

The series was born out of an understanding that practitioners want information and guidance about improving teaching and learning that is *relevant to them* – rooted in their particular subject, and applicable to pupils they encounter. These books exactly fulfil that function.

Those original books have stood the test of time in many ways – their tried and tested, practical strategies are as relevant and effective as ever. Legislation and national guidance have moved on, however, as have resources and technology; new terminology accompanies all of these changes. For example, we have changed the series title to incorporate the acronym 'SEND' (Special Educational Needs or Disability) which has been adopted in official documents and in many schools in response to recent legislation and the revised Code of Practice. The important point to make is that our authors have addressed the needs of pupils with a wide range of special or 'additional' needs; some will have Educational, Health and Care (EHC) plans which have replaced 'statements', but most will not. Some will have identified 'syndromes' or 'conditions' but many will simply be termed 'low attainers', pupils who, for whatever reason, do not easily make progress.

This second edition encompasses recent developments in education, and specifically in music teaching. At the time of publication, education is still very much in an era of change; our national curriculum, monitoring and assessment systems are all newly fashioned and many schools are still adjusting to changes and developing their own ways forward. The ideas and guidance contained in this book, however, transcend the fluctuations of national politics and policy and provide a framework for ensuring that pupils with SEND can 'enjoy and achieve' in their music lessons.

Linda D. Evans

Preface

Children and young people are surrounded, often bombarded, by music every day of their lives. As teachers and music educators our role is to help them develop a deeper understanding of what music is and how it works; to know why they enjoy particular kinds of music, and to explore music they may otherwise not have encountered. We do that through engaging them in active listening, composition and improvisation, and making and controlling sounds. Some children and young people will develop high levels of skill as music-makers, while others find it more challenging and benefit from a less active role.

Teachers and music educators working with those who have additional needs may face challenges in their working environment for which they have not been prepared. The down-to-earth advice this book provides, along with its mixture of factual information and helpful hints, supports everyone in this situation. The increase in self-confidence and self-esteem that comes from participation in music-making often helps learners to overcome difficulties in other parts of their life, both in and out of school. The authors, both long-serving classroom practitioners, know this from personal experience, and it is this understanding that has enabled them to provide authoritative yet friendly guidance in this user-friendly volume.

Richard Crozier
MA, BAHons, PGCE
co-author of *The Music Teacher's Companion*

Acknowledgements

The authors and publishers would like to thank:

* Mavis West and Jan Holdstock for their inspiration and experience;
* all their friends at YAMSEN (the Yorkshire Association for Music and Special Educational Needs), especially the late Gordon Parry, for their support, encouragement and belief;
* Charlotte Emery for her pictures;
* all those pupils and teachers in Leeds who we worked with;
* Bob Spooner for his belief in Victoria;
* the Drake Music Project for teaching Diane the ropes of enabling music technology;
* Colin Brackley-Jones for creating our working partnership;
* Sally Zimmerman and the RNIB for advice and encouragement for Diane;
* Mick Pitchford for inspirational training;
* Catherine J. Stockdale for kick-starting us;
* Lee Boyes for keeping us going when we started to droop;
* Anne Hewitt for her tireless support and reading the original draft;
* Karen Ruzicka, Sheila Hardwick and Yvonne Smith for their advice;
* Natalie, Xanthe and Janet for sharing their ideas;
* both our families for their patience in the face of neglect;
* Rick for his continuous support and cooking;
* Joanna, Chloe, Fehmina, Suzanne and Christopher for their contributions and IT support.

The authors and publishers would also like to thank:

* David Evans of Fox Lane Photography;
* staff and pupils of St John's CoE Middle School in Bromsgrove and Queensbury School in Erdington for allowing us to use their photographs;
* OcPix™ copyright © 1988 D&C Liggins – www.ocarina.co.uk.

Introduction

Ours to teach

Your class: thirty individuals to teach – to encourage, motivate and inspire: thirty individuals who must be seen to make good progress regardless of their various abilities, backgrounds, interests and personalities. This is what makes teaching so interesting!

Jason demonstrates very little interest in school. He rarely completes homework and frequently turns up without a pen. He finds it hard to listen when you're talking or playing music and is likely to start his own conversation with a classmate. His work is untidy and mostly incomplete. It's difficult to find evidence of his progress this year.

Zoe tries very hard in lessons but is slow to understand explanations and has difficulty in expressing herself. She has been assessed as having poor communication skills but there is no additional resourcing for her.

Ethan is on the autistic spectrum and finds it difficult to relate to other people, to work in a group and to understand social norms. He has an Education, Health and Care plan which provides for some TA support but this is not timetabled for all lessons.

Do you recognise these youngsters? Our school population is now more diverse than ever before, with pupils of very different abilities, aptitudes and interests, from a wide range of cultures, making up our mainstream and special school classes. Many of these learners will experience difficulties of some sort at school, especially when they are faced with higher academic expectations at the end of KS2 and into KS3 to 4.

Whether they have a specific special educational need like dyslexia, or are on the autistic spectrum, or for various reasons cannot conform to our behavioural expectations – *they are ours to teach*. Our lessons must ensure that each and every pupil can develop their skills and knowledge and make good progress.

How can this book help?

The information, ideas and guidance in this book will enable teachers of Music (and their teaching assistants) to plan and deliver lessons that will meet the individual needs of learners who experience difficulties. It will be especially valuable to subject teachers because the ideas and guidance are provided within a subject context, ensuring relevance and practicability.

Teachers who cater well for pupils with special educational needs and disabilities (SEND) are likely to cater well for *all* pupils – demonstrating outstanding practice in their everyday teaching. These teachers have a keen awareness of the many factors affecting a pupil's ability to learn, not only characteristics of the individual but also aspects of the learning environment that can either help or hinder learning. This book will help practitioners to develop strategies that can be used selectively to enable each and every learner to make progress.

Professional development

Our education system is constantly changing. The national curriculum, SEND legislation, examination reform and significant change to Ofsted inspection mean that teachers need to keep up to date and be able to develop the knowledge, skills and understanding necessary to meet the needs of all the learners they teach. High quality continuing professional development (CPD) has a big part to play in this.

Faculties and subject teams planning for outstanding teaching and learning should consider how they regularly review and improve their provision by:

- auditing
    a) the skills and expertise of current staff (teachers and assistants)
    b) their professional development needs for SEND, based on the current cohorts of pupils;
    (There is an audit proforma on the accompanying website: www.routledge. com/9781138231849.)

- using the information from the two audits to develop a CPD programme (using internal staff, colleagues from nearby schools and/or consultants to deliver bespoke training);

- enabling teachers to observe each other, teach together, visit other class-rooms and other schools;
- encouraging staff to reflect on their practice and feel comfortable in sharing both the positive and the negative experiences;
- establishing an ethos that values everyone's expertise (including pupils and parents/carers who might be able to contribute to training sessions);
- using online resources that are readily available to support workforce development (e.g. www.nasen.org.uk/onlinesendcpd/);
- encouraging staff to access (and disseminate) further study and high quality professional development.

This book, and the others in the series, will be invaluable in contributing to whole-school CPD on meeting special educational needs, and in facilitating subject-specific staff development within departments.

1 Meeting special educational needs

Your responsibility

New legislation and national guidance in 2014 changed the landscape of educational provision for pupils with any sort of 'additional' or 'special' needs. The vast majority of learners, including those with 'moderate' or 'mild' learning difficulties, weak communication skills, dyslexia or social/behavioural needs, rarely attract additional resources: they are very much accepted as part of the 'mainstream mix'. Pupils with more significant special educational needs and/or disabilities (SEND) may have an education, health and care plan (EHC plan): this outlines how particular needs will be met, often involving professionals from different disciplines, and sometimes specifying adult support in the classroom. Both groups of pupils are ultimately the responsibility of the class teacher, whether in mainstream or special education.

> High quality teaching that is differentiated and personalised will meet the individual needs of the majority of children and young people. Some children and young people need educational provision that is additional to or different from this. This is special educational provision under Section 21 of the Children and Families Act 2014. Schools and colleges *must* use their best endeavours to ensure that such provision is made for those who need it. Special educational provision is underpinned by high quality teaching and is compromised by anything less.
>
> SEND Code of Practice 2015

There is more information about legislation (the Children and Families Act 2014; the Equality Act 2010) and guidance (SEND Code of Practice) in Appendix 1.

Definition of SEND

A pupil has special educational needs if he or she:

- has a significantly greater difficulty in learning than the majority of others of the same age; or

- has a disability which prevents or hinders him or her from making use of facilities of a kind generally provided for others of the same age in mainstream schools or mainstream post-16 institutions.

(SEND Code of Practice 2015)

The SEND Code of Practice identifies four broad areas of SEND, but remember that this gives only an overview of the range of needs that should be planned for by schools; pupils' needs rarely fit neatly into one area of need only.

Table 1.1 The four broad areas of SEND

Communication and interaction	Cognition and learning	Social, emotional and mental health difficulties	Sensory and/or physical needs
Speech, language and communication needs (SLCN)

Asperger's syndrome and autism (ASD) | Specific learning difficulties (SpLD)

Moderate learning difficulties (MLD)

Severe learning difficulties (SLD)

Profound and multiple learning difficulties (PMLD) | Mental health difficulties such as anxiety or depression, self-harming, substance abuse or eating disorders

Attention deficit disorders, attention deficit hyperactivity disorder or attachment disorder | Vision impairment (VI)

Hearing impairment (HI)

Multi-sensory impairment (MSI)

Physical disability (PD) |

Whole school ethos

Successful schools are proactive in identifying and addressing pupils' special needs, focusing on adapting the educational context and environment rather than on 'fixing' an individual learner. Adapting systems and teaching programmes rather than trying to force the pupil to conform to rigid expectations will lead to a greater chance of success in terms of learning outcomes. Guidance on whole school and departmental policy making can be found in Appendix 2 and a sample departmental policy for SEND can be downloaded from our website: www.routledge.com/9781138231849.

Policy into practice

In many cases, pupils' individual learning needs will be met through differentiation of tasks and materials in their lessons; sometimes this will be supplemented by targeted interventions such as literacy 'catch-up' programmes delivered outside the classroom. A smaller number of pupils may need access to more specialist equipment and approaches, perhaps based on advice and support from external specialists.

The main thrust of the Children and Families Act and Chapter 6 of the SEND Code of Practice is that outcomes for pupils with SEN must be improved and that schools and individual teachers must have high aspirations and expectations for all.

In practice, this means that pupils should be enabled to:

- **achieve their best**; additional provision made for pupils with SEN will enable them to make accelerated progress so that the gap in progress and attainment between them and other pupils is reduced. Being identified with SEN should no longer be a reason for a pupil making less than good progress.
- **become confident individuals living fulfilling lives**; if you ask parents/carers of children with SEN what is important to them for their child's future, they often answer 'happiness, the opportunity to achieve his or her potential, friendships, and a loving family' – just what we all want for our children. Outcomes in terms of well-being, social skills and growing independence are equally as important as academic outcomes for children and young people with SEND.
- **make a successful transition into adulthood, whether into employment, further or higher education or training**; decisions made at transition from primary school, in Year 7 and beyond should be made in the context of preparation for adulthood. For example, where a pupil has had full-time support from a teaching assistant in primary school, the secondary school's first reaction might be to continue this level of support after transition. This may result in long-term dependency on adults, however, or limited opportunities to develop social skills, both of which impact negatively on preparation for adulthood.

Excellent classroom provision

Throughout this book you will find lots of subject-specific ideas and guidance on strategies to support pupils with SEND, but there are some generic approaches that form the foundations of outstanding provision, such as:

- providing support from adults or other pupils;
- adapting tasks or environments;
- using specialist aids and equipment as appropriate.

The starting points listed below provide a sound basis for creating an inclusive learning environment that will benefit *all* pupils, while being especially important for those with SEND.

Develop pupils' understanding through the use of all available senses by:

- using resources that pupils can access through sight AND sound (and where appropriate also use the senses of touch, taste and smell to broaden understanding and ensure stronger memory);
- regularly employing resources such as symbols, pictures and film to increase pupils' knowledge of the wider world and contextualise new information and skills;
- encouraging and enabling pupils to take part in activities such as play, drama, choirs, bands, visual arts, sports, class visits and exploring the environment.

Help pupils to learn effectively and prepare for further or higher education, work or training by:

- setting realistic demands within high expectations;
- using positive strategies to manage behaviour;
- giving pupils opportunities and encouragement to develop the skills to work effectively in a group or with a partner;
- teaching all pupils to value and respect the contribution of others;
- encouraging independent working skills;
- teaching essential safety rules.

Help pupils to develop communication skills, language and literacy by:

- giving clear, step-by step instructions, and limiting the amount of information given at one time;
- providing a list of key vocabulary for each lesson;
- choosing texts that pupils can read and understand;
- making texts available in different formats, including large text, symbols or by using screen reader programs;
- putting headings and important points in bold or highlighting to make them easier to scan;
- presenting written information as concisely as possible, using bullet points, images or diagrams.

Support pupils with disabilities by:

- encouraging pupils to be as independent as possible;
- enabling them to work with other, non-disabled pupils;
- making sure the classroom environment is suitable, e.g. uncluttered space to facilitate movement around the classroom or lab; adapted resources that are labelled and accessible;

- being aware that some pupils will take longer to complete tasks, including homework;
- taking into account the higher levels of concentration and physical exertion required by some pupils (even in activities such as reading and writing) that will lead to increased fatigue for pupils who may already have reduced stamina;
- being aware of the extra effort required by some pupils to follow oral work, whether through use of residual hearing, lip reading or signed support, and of the tiredness and limited concentration which is likely to ensue;
- ensuring all pupils are included, and can participate safely, in school trips and off-site visits.

These and other, more specific, strategies are placed in the context of supporting particular individuals such as those described in the case studies in Appendix 3.

2 Starting points

This chapter is a starting point for information on the special educational needs most frequently encountered in mainstream schools. It describes the main characteristics of each area of special educational need and disability (SEND) with practical ideas for use in music lessons.

There is a measure of repetition, as some strategies prove to be effective with a whole range of pupils (and often with those who have no identified SEND!). However, the layout enables readers an 'at a glance' reminder of effective approaches and facilitates copying for colleagues and TAs. (Please see Appendix 3 for detailed case studies of individual pupils and the provision made for them in music.)

The SEND Code of Practice (Department for Education, 2014) outlines four broad areas of need. These are:

- communication and interaction;
- cognition and learning;
- social, emotional and mental health difficulties;
- sensory and/or physical needs.

These broad areas are not exclusive and pupils may have needs that cut across some or all of them. Equally, pupils' difficulties and needs will change over time. The terms used in this chapter are helpful when reviewing and monitoring special educational provision, but pupils' individual talents and interests are just as important as their disability or special educational need. Because of this, specific terms or labels need to be used with care in discussion with parents, pupils or other professionals. Unless a pupil has a firm diagnosis, and parents and pupil understand the implications of that diagnosis, it is more appropriate to describe the features of the special educational need rather than use the label. For example, a teacher might describe a pupil's spelling difficulties but not use the term 'dyslexic'.

There is a continuum of need within each of the special educational needs and disabilities listed here. Some pupils will be affected more than others, and show fewer or more of the characteristics described.

Pupils with other, less common special educational needs may be included in some schools, and additional information on these conditions may be found in a variety of sources. These include the school SENCO, local authority support services, educational psychologists and online information, for example on the NASEN SEND Gateway and disability charity websites such as Mencap, CAF or I CAN, the Children's Communication Charity.

www.nasen.org.uk
www.mencap.org.uk
www.cafamily.org.uk
www.ican.org.uk

Figure 2.1 Lionel never felt the need to sit down.

The autistic spectrum including Asperger's syndrome and semantic pragmatic disorder

Intro	Pupils on the autistic spectrum often have perfect pitch (with all the hazards that that brings!), and some may be savants. They may already be obsessed with certain genres of music. A problem these pupils have is that their creative musical imagination may be in advance of their physical musical ability. Also they cannot handle overstimulation of the senses.
Ways in	Find out as soon as you can what, if any, musical obsessions they have, and then over time assess whether to use them, develop them further or avoid encouraging them.
Teaching and learning	It's not easy to generalise about teaching and learning approaches. High functioning students may use conventional notation; at the other end of the scale, pupils will need PECS (Picture Exchange Communication System) and intensive interaction, musical interaction and music therapy. Explain carefully in advance, either verbally or in pictures, what activity is going to happen next, and leave them to get there in their time.
Room layout	People on the autistic spectrum like routines and would appreciate having the same desk every week. To avoid over-stimulating the senses, have the wall that they sit opposite free of all display, and have a time out where they can retreat if the sounds become overwhelming.
NB/Comment	Don't be upset if pupils with autism put their hands over their ears. They may be upset with poor quality or out of tune instruments (perhaps over time the music department may replace them!). Also they may not appear to be taking note of the lessons, but they will be. See the example below.
Anecdote/ case study	Every week, all year round, Diane would sing her goodbye song. Most of the pupils joined in. Adrian didn't. Then one week Diane made a mistake in the song, and Adrian stared at her in disbelief.

The National Autistic Society www.autism.org.uk
Autism Education Trust www.autismeducationtrust.org.uk
PECS www.pecs.com

Social, emotional and mental health difficulties (including ADHD)

Intro	Pupils with social, emotional and mental health difficulties that present challenging behaviour jeopardise their own musical achievement, but may also affect everyone else's. Whether they have significant needs and are supported by an EHC plan or are 'just naughty' or 'disaffected', these learners can pose real challenges in music lessons.
Ways in	It helps if all lessons follow a clear routine and are pacy. This is good behaviour management anyway, but essential in this case. And now is the time for initial low academic expectations! In the first instance the teacher needs to concentrate on setting rules and creating a calm environment. At first, success will be measured simply by how calm and cooperative your students are, but quite quickly you will usually be rewarded by pleasing musical progress.
Teaching and learning	In whole class situations, following conventional notation may be difficult, but pupils who are challenging are also often gifted, so you shouldn't rule it out. However, in general these students are impatient and will prefer practical trial and error.
Room layout	No special arrangements, but best to place the students with challenging behaviour somewhere near the door or the edge of the room, so that they can be removed with as little fuss as possible, should it come to it.
NB	Including pupils with challenging behaviour in the class requires an infinite set of tactics and a lot of patience. Discussing their behaviour with them is pointless, and if you do it during the lesson, it adversely affects the other students' education. (However, it is depressingly certain that you will blow your best laid plans at some point!) It is important, though, not to appear to ignore any inappropriate behaviour and thereby confuse other students; make it clear that you will follow it up at some point. Report cards often work well.

SEBDA, Social, Emotional and Behavioural Difficulties Association www.sebda.org

www.youngminds.org.uk

The National Attention Deficit Disorder Information and Support Service www.addiss.co.uk

Blindness and visual impairment

Intro	It is important to discover how visually impaired the student is from the outset. After that, music is the one subject where the student with VI has an equal chance of success. We strongly recommend that they take GCSE Music.
Ways in	Don't overdo the obvious support. Let the student find her/his way around the music room, and make a time when the others are working to discuss any help you can offer. Most importantly, you must avoid sudden loud noises.
Teaching and learning	Conventional notation is probably out, but, for those with some sight, you can provide enlarged worksheets; Braille music is available but time-consuming, maybe good for one-to-one work; learning aurally is the most logical method.
Room layout	Make the room easy to manoeuvre around, and best to keep tables etc. in the same place all year.
NB/Comment	If the blind child is a savant, you may expect a certain type of musical genius. You must provide opportunities for them to improve and to perform publicly, but take care not to make a fuss at the expense of the rest of the class.
Anecdote/ case study	A music educator was at a summer school in Country X where a blind teenage savant played his party piece for everyone in the final concert. It was absolutely beautiful and moved him and all the audience to tears. Two years passed and the same educator was at another music education conference, where the same savant played the same piece but not as well. He stopped to consider the implications.

Royal National Institute for Blind People, RNIB www.rnib.org.uk

Dyspraxia

Intro	Students with dyspraxia may appear slow and clumsy but they are capable of succeeding at any instrument they choose. They need a diagnosis and a teacher with faith in them.
Ways in	How you approach a student with dyspraxia may well depend on how old they are and how much they are aware of their condition. In the case study below Tanya had a determined parent and a supportive teacher, and had got to the age and the point where a diagnosis was a relief.
Teaching and learning	For GCSE Music you might consider asking for extra time in the written exam.
Room layout	No special arrangements needed.
Comment	When pupils with dyspraxia know that a task is not beyond them, and yet they don't get there as quickly as their classmates, they may despair and lose self-esteem.
Anecdote/ case study	Tanya was at a private school; her older sister had already got a place at Oxbridge, but Tanya was in bottom sets for everything. Then in her Year 10 she got a new geography teacher, who, out of the blue, asked if she had been tested for dyspraxia. The diagnosis boosted her self-belief and Tanya achieved A grades at GCSE and at A level, followed by first-class honours at Birmingham University in Biology, a PGCSE in primary school teaching from Cambridge, and a PhD in Maths for Pupils with Additional Needs. She achieved Grade 8 with the saxophone and has played with an award-winning band at the Royal Albert Hall for Music for Youth.

Dyspraxia Foundation www.dyspraxiafoundation.org.uk

Dyslexia and dyscalculia

Intro	Students with dyslexia/dyscalculia should flourish in Music, given a little 'TLC', as it is perfectly possible for them to play an instrument without reading any notations. These pupils may arrive in the Music lesson despondent and with low self-esteem, however, as a result of the negative feedback that weak basic skills in literacy and numeracy can attract.
Ways in	Any instrument may be suitable. Watch out for students using avoidance tactics or exhibiting challenging behaviour.
Teaching and learning	Limit how much written information is on the board and read out loud any text that you use; avoid written work as much as possible and provide a spell-checker for essential written assignments. Use multi-sensory/kinaesthetic approaches as much as possible. For GCSE Music you might consider asking for extra time in a timed assignment.
	See the British Dyslexia Association for more information (as below).
Room layout	No special arrangements needed.
NB/Comment	Anecdotally there are many famous artists, musicians and entrepreneurs who are dyslexic (see 'A Pianist's Story' by Jill Backhouse on the BDA website, www.bdadyslexia.org.uk/educator/music-and-dyslexia) but they often speak of how miserable they were at school, and how they avoided situations they found embarrassing to the point of exhibiting challenging behaviour and truanting. Music and the Arts should be the lessons where poor spelling and/or weak numeracy are not an issue.

British Dyslexia Association www.bdadyslexia.org.uk
The Dyslexia Association www.dyslexia.uk.net

Deafness and hearing impairment

Intro	Deaf pupils and those with a hearing impairment can clearly see what everyone else is doing and usually want to do the same. They may or may not realise that the actions they are seeing have corresponding sounds. While they can play the correct notes, they may miss out on such things as rhythmic accuracy, quiet dynamics and expressive subtleties.
Ways in	By watching the other students and the teacher, some instruments are very quickly accessible, especially wooden percussion. Wooden sounds die away quickly and don't leave a confusing cacophony of vibrations. Xylophones and djembes are good, and we also recommend tamboo bamboo (wooden or plastic on the floor).
Teaching and learning	If the rest of the class are using notation, there is no reason not to use it with pupils who have HI. Take care that any visual displays are within students' sightline. Ask TAs to check that hearing aids are correctly adjusted.
Room layout	Pupils with HI may use lip reading and facial expressions to help them understand what is being said, so make sure they are positioned where they can see you, the teacher, at all times and if possible everyone else in the room.
NB	It is easy for pupils with HI to knock instruments out of tune, and for them to irritate other students by sounding insensitively loud. Make sure that you devise some signs for dynamics. Learn a few key signs, e.g. for loud, quiet, stop, etc.
	Be careful that any signers don't come between teacher and pupils and pupils and other pupils.
	Make sure that no one approaches or touches a deaf child without warning.
	With greater incidence of cochlea implants, there are fewer pupils who experience total deafness.
Anecdote/ case study	School X included a deaf unit for primary school pupils with HI. Three boys in Year 5 were rightly included in the music lesson, but signing everything that the music teacher said to the class was affecting the atmosphere, the pace of the lesson and the relationship that the music teacher wanted to develop with the boys. The signers and she decided to reverse the order of things, and until the end of this particular course they conducted the lessons in absolute silence (i.e. without any verbal input). And it worked.

Action on Hearing Loss www.actiononhearingloss.org.uk
The National Deaf Children's Society www.ndcs.org.uk

Moderate learning difficulties

Intro	At first, pupils with MLD seem to be able to cope; they are willing to try anything out, are quite brave, not shy. But these pupils usually (not always) plateau quite quickly, and unless the teacher is prepared for this, the students will lose heart. On the other hand, you may find that some pupils with MLD respond apparently disproportionately to music, and may 'shine'.
Ways in	You may start the same as for everyone in the class, trying out all instruments, but ones with notes with big surface areas are really suitable, such as djembes, marimbas, gamelan. Single chime bars or big bass chime bars are good, as is singing, but you must differentiate carefully and nurture any signs of ability. It's usually better that the students with MLD are not taking parts to themselves but that they always double up with other players.
Teaching and learning	Conventional notation will probably be too hard. Very simple songs in Foxwood notation would be okay, but learning notes and rhythms aurally is best.
Room layout	No special arrangements needed.
NB	Students are usually (often) very enthusiastic about learning music, but a careless word or action can easily damage their self-esteem.
Anecdote/ case study	Harry, now in his forties, can play any instrument that he takes up after only a few days – clarinet, accordion, piano, drum kit, etc. He likes to have a copy of the music – but sometimes it can be seen to be upside down. However, he plays beautifully by ear, and always plays along with the mainstream bands that accompany the various inclusive concerts that he attends.

Down's Syndrome Association www.downs-syndrome.org.uk

Physical disability

Intro	It could be said that students with a physical difficulty fall into two groups: those who have no other additional needs will require nothing more than spaces for their wheelchairs or other walking aids to move easily around, and instruments that they can reach. If the difficulty is in the upper body, they may need instruments adapted for their use. There is a tendency for able-bodied people, sadly including school staff, to assume all sorts of other complications for wheelchair users.
	Pupils with more significant disabilities which result in them being barely able to move can access music through technology. They will often have communication aids, which get more sophisticated by the month/year, whose only drawback is that they can physically come between teacher and student, and student and instrument.
Ways in	The teacher must find out what a student with PD can do and how they will be able to do it. The carer will know the latter, but possibly not in relation to music.
Teaching and learning	Pupils can benefit from technology such as switches, iPads, soundbeams, etc.
Room layout	It is essential that doors are wide enough, aisles are free of clutter, displays are low enough and instruments are accessible.
Anecdote/ case study	Karl loves making his own music but can only do this by using two head switches or moving his head in front of a soundbeam. He can communicate using these head switches through his computer, but sometimes when using switches to play music this needs to be removed to enable him to see the rest of the group. His favourite music is heavy metal. He writes his own poems, which can be very dark in meaning, and then sets these to music. He has performed in concerts using these switches, working with the Gordon Parry Centre Team at Artforms. Playing in ensembles has been difficult, however, as he is not used to sharing the space.

Scope www.scope.org.uk

Students with PMLD (profound and multiple learning difficulties)

Intro	Pupils with PMLD are rarely placed in a mainstream school; if they are, it will be with a full-time carer. They may have virtually no movement, but they can benefit from well-planned music lessons. These students need to be offered a variety of musical experiences, especially live ones, and the opportunity to produce their own sounds, and to be part of the music ensemble and social group.
Ways in	Teaching students with PMLD requires a multi-sensory approach. Most of the work will be done one-to-one by their regular carer, but the music teacher needs to provide the opportunities in the form of instruments and music technology. (Make sure that the assistant doesn't hold or grab the student's arms to make them play. Supporting from beneath the elbow is most effective in giving support but also allowing for some independence.)
Teaching and learning	For pupils with PMLD, mostly it is a case of discovering what they can relate to, or actually do for themselves. You may need to repeat activities over the course of a term in order to discover what works. Again the carers will know their charges well and their support in music lessons will be invaluable.
Room layout	Basically there needs to be space for a wheelchair (or custom made transporter) and instruments to be accessible.
NB/Comment	Teachers shouldn't assume that because they can't see a reaction from their students it is not happening. It will be the carers who identify when the students are engaged.
Anecdote/ case study	One of our pupils was upset by the sound of other children in the class, crying as a result. Besides his other difficulties, he was blind; he regularly wore headphones, but in one-to-one sessions he grew to like a gathering drum held over his head and whacked as loudly as possible.

Mencap www.mencap.org.uk

Foundation for People with Learning Disabilities www.learningdisabilities. org.uk

Tourette's syndrome

Intro	Like stutterers, pupils with Tourette's syndrome can lose all their symptoms when singing or involved in music. If they appear in your music lesson in their tutor group or with a group of friends, they usually exhibit fewer tics and swear less, because they are among friends. Sometimes, however, they can be wound up by insensitive teachers or pupils with behaviour problems. Stress is the trigger, so take care not to pressurise these pupils in any way (until you know them better).
Ways in	Firstly, know about the syndrome before you meet the student and brace yourself not to react to the profanities. They can just take you by surprise. Keep the teacher talk to a minimum and move onto practical work as quickly as possible.
Teaching and learning	Establish a good relationship with the student and agree on an 'escape route' if the tics become too disruptive or distressing.
Room layout	No special layout needed, but the student may prefer to sit at the back of the room where s/he is not in everyone's line of sight (ask him/her).
NB/Comment	Other students, in my experience, support and protect their peers with Tourette's. They go out of their way not to react to the swearing, but address any teasing and bullying straight away.
Anecdote/ case study	Kris was a talented musician and was sent to the peripatetic's lesson in a small group with four other students, none of whom were in the same tutor group or even school year. It was an unusual and unfortunate mix of students as two others tended to challenging behaviour and (even worse) the lessons were conducted in a large cupboard, with no natural daylight or even a window in the door.

Kris had learned a tune from another teacher and spent some weeks playing it, refusing to learn anything else or play along with the others. His swearing and tics got worse, and he chewed quite a few drumsticks. By the end of the term all but one of the students was left in the class, and the peripatetic teacher's mental health was in melt down, despite her being an SEN Music specialist. |

Tourettes Action UK www.tourettes-action.org.uk

3 The inclusive music classroom

The physical state of the classroom is important for all pupils, but especially wheelchair users, pupils with visual impairments and those on the autistic spectrum. In this chapter we will consider the physical layout and attributes of the music room, from space to storage, furniture and display.

The position of the music department within the school building may not be negotiable, but it is worth mentioning that, for best use, it should be situated where lessons can go on – unimpeded – all school day long, all year round, whatever other activities are happening within the school. Where music departments have their rooms close to the school hall in order to facilitate performances such as school concerts and assembly contributions, they inevitably find themselves close to the exam room (which is also the school hall) and unable to make any noise for a significant amount of time.

Figure 3.1 Quiet please, there's an exam going on next door.

Ideally the music department should be a suite of soundproof carpeted rooms, one of which can be used as a recording studio. It should be located on the ground floor, possibly next to the drama studio, as part of a performing arts suite. The main performance or large practice area should have appropriate acoustics. If this space is a ghastly echo chamber, then there are ways of improving the sound using curtains and professional baffling (see the research of Adrian James, a government adviser on acoustics). Good acoustics are important for everyone but absolutely vital for those with hearing impairment.

Between each room in the music suite there should be triple-glazed glass/per-spex (studio quality) windows. The biggest room should contain a low stage, with a ramp up from both sides. There should be one or two large teaching rooms, a large performance room, a private, staff-only office, and several smaller store cupboards and practice rooms. One of these smaller rooms can double as a retreat or 'time-out' room, a quiet space where pupils can work individually or in a pair. This room should be big enough for a wheelchair and one or two pupils, plus an adult. The door should have a window so that the teacher can monitor the pupils' work even when the door is closed (and of

Figure 3.2 The use of baffling to improve acoustics.

course protect any student or adult in terms of any safe-guarding issues). This sort of room can also act as a recording studio.

Furniture

At least some of the desks and tables should be adjustable and arranged in a way which allows for **wheelchair users and blind students** to move easily around the room. Stools are a good seating option, and they allow space for pupils who use wheelchairs, crutches or other mobility aids. However, some pupils with motor co-ordination difficulties will need the security of a chair back. It is vital that desks and keyboards are not fixed to the floor and are centrally located. One minute a music room can be an orchestra, the next it could be a marching samba band! A local colleague has recently got rid of the desks altogether and starts all her lessons with students sitting round in a circle before they go into breakout spaces and to the keyboard benches.

It goes without saying that a clean and tidy room benefits all. It saves so much time in lessons if glockenspiel beaters are in a box marked 'glockenspiel beaters'. Plus, if they are always put away after use and not left out, there's less chance of losing any. Working in an untidy room, apart from slowing everything down, would upset the **students on the autistic spectrum**, and make it hard for them to concentrate on their work.

Instrument storage

There should be enough rooms/space to leave drum kits, steel pans and keyboards set up and in place. Violins, violas and all brass and woodwind instruments should be stored in their cases. Guitars, cellos and double basses may be in cases, or safely put in custom made racks. Glockenspiels and xylophones etc. should be in neat rows on shelves. Untuned small percussion should be in trolleys or boxes. Congas and timbales etc. should be available to use, i.e. not cased up all the time, but put discreetly to one side. Decks are best set up in a locked studio.

In general, the more delicate and the smaller the instrument, the more it needs to be stored in a case when not being played. Drum kits should always be set up, and one should always be set up for left-handed users. Percussion instruments in particular are prone to people tapping them as they pass (this includes staff). Sticks and beaters need to be kept to one side in boxes.

Personal belongings

It is useful to have coat racks in the main teaching room: most pupils like to keep their coats in sight and this allows them to be stored tidily. Providing a safe place for bags also avoids cluttering up the teaching area and minimises the risk of anyone tripping over – particularly important for pupils with dyspraxia.

There should be a no-go area around the teacher's desk. The central controls to turn the keyboards on and off, and also the sound systems and video, will be here. This is where the teacher can look after pupils' personal possessions. The keyboard wires and the headphone splitters can also be kept here. Here too should be all the pens and pencils. No lesson should ever be held up because a child has not got a pen, and the once-a-week music lesson is not the place to fight over a child's stationery responsibilities.

Technical support

Music departments benefit considerably from having a technician, whether for just a few hours a week or full time. This person can check over and repair the headphones, the keyboards, iPads, etc. on a weekly basis. They should tune the guitars and all other stringed instruments and replace worn strings. How much lesson time is lost both by peripatetic teachers and by classroom teachers in tuning up instruments or looking round for working headphones? Have spare keyboard electrical leads available so that no keyboards are ever out of action.

The technician should put the keys back on the xylophones and glockenspiels, generally stack and tidy, get rid of broken items and advise on replacements. Technicians can also record exam performances, act as sound engineers for evening concerts and make visual records – including some for the school website.

Display

Display should:

- be relevant
- be interesting
- be up-to-date
- be well-presented and
- include pupils' own work.

There should be key words, placed in some sort of logical order, on a wall or a board or on a screen. They could be changed monthly, weekly, daily or even, if it makes the difference that the teacher needs, for each lesson. Indeed, the latter would suit children with hearing impairments or learning difficulties as they would benefit from having available additional visual information linked to the lesson. Be aware that, for pupils with autistic spectrum disorder, busy, colourful displays can prove overstimulating; being allowed to sit near to or facing a plain wall can help them to remain focused on the lesson.

Music can reflect children's own culture and society, and classroom displays can be a place to showcase their favourite artists. Apart from obviously being an opportunity to display musicians and instruments from different ethnic minorities, and to portray women and girls in a positive way, the wall display is where we can put on show artists with disabilities. If the disability is not obvious, an explanatory sentence can make it so. (Suitable artists for this might be Stevie Wonder and Itzhak Perlman.)

Give consideration to the height of displays – wheelchair users will have a lower eye level than their peers – and make sure that lettering is as big and bold as possible so that pupils with less than perfect vision can still read it.

Give careful consideration to writing over picture backgrounds as this can make text very difficult to read, particularly for those with visual impairment.

Photographs can also be effective in the production of 'visual instructions' – particularly useful for hearing-impaired and autistic students. If you use photographs of pupils in displays, permission should be obtained from parents or carers. Also you must consider the effect on the pupils featured (and on those not used in pictures) in terms of self-esteem.

Literacy in music lessons

Information sheets and listening and activity sheets will be used from time to time and it's important to remember that some pupils will have limited literacy skills. If pupils are asked to research on the internet, they may well be faced with material that is difficult to read and understand. Pairing these students with a partner or 'buddy' who is a competent reader can help them to develop their reading skills generally, as well as ensure that they understand the content of any particular piece of information.

When designing your own activity or information sheets, keep the content simple and concise (remembering that shorter sentences do not necessarily make for easier understanding). Avoid passive constructions, e.g. 'The 1812 Overture was composed by Tchaikovsky', as these may confuse pupils; 'Tchaikovsky composed the 1812 Overture' is easier to grasp. (Table 3.1 gives ideas for checking the accessibility of written material and producing your own information/question sheets.)

Word banks provide effective support for pupils with weak literacy skills and should be on display in the music room.

Table 3.1 Guidelines for writing question sheets

Fonts	Arial, Universe and New Century Schoolbook are easier to read than other fonts.
Font size	12 or 14 is best for most pupils.
Font format	**Bold** is OK; *italic* is hard to read.
Layout	Use lots of headings and subheadings as signposts, leave lots of space between lines and paragraphs.
CAPITAL LETTERS	These are hard to read so use sparingly.
Consistency	Ensure instructions and symbols are used consistently.
Provide answers	If pupils can check answers (to closed questions) for themselves, they learn more and become more independent.
Enlarging	It is better to enlarge text by using a bigger font on a word processor rather than relying on the photocopier. Photocopied enlargements can appear fuzzy and A3 paper never fits neatly in exercise books or folders.
Forms	If you are making an answer sheet or cloze exercise, remember that partially sighted pupils often have handwriting that is larger than average, so allow extra space on forms. This will also help pupils with learning difficulties who have immature or poorly formed writing or are still printing.
Spacing	Keep to the same amount of space between each word. Do not use justified text as the uneven word spacing can make reading more difficult.
Alignment	Align text to the left margin. This makes it easer to find the start and finish of each line. It ensures an even space between each word.
Placing illustrations	Do not wrap text around images if it means that lines of text will start in different places. Do not have text going over images as this makes it hard to read.

Conclusion

The status of music in the school curriculum changes with each change of government and education minister. Without wishing to become political, we can't emphasise enough how vital music is for the educational and personal development of every one of us.

New-build high schools tend to include sophisticated gadgets and expensive electronic equipment, but too often they have insufficient space for world instruments and practice rooms that are too small, especially for wheelchair users. Apart from being unsuitable for wheelchair users or a student and a TA as well as the teacher, spending so much time in such a small room will begin to adversely affect the visiting teacher's health.

And so, whether it is an imperfect new-build or a draughty old building, music teachers will always have to work with what they have, and fight for more. What are the most important things that an inclusive classroom should contain in order that children with additional needs can get the most from their lessons? Here is our wish list:

- enough space for wheelchairs and mobility aids
- all equipment at an accessible level
- clear pathways (for those pupils with VI and/or limited mobility)
- a comfortable acoustic (especially for pupils with HI and ASD)
- some blank walls (for pupils on the autistic spectrum)
- easily accessible resources (books and IT) to enable the teacher to keep the pace moving.

4 Instruments

Inevitably the music room that a teacher inherits will not include all the instruments that they might have chosen (it's always worth checking out if there are any 'gems' hidden on the shelves waiting for a good dusting down).

In this chapter we will consider what instruments you are likely to find, or even to buy, and how they may suit students with special/additional needs. Whatever you do buy, ensure that it is a proper professional instrument, and not a toy. (The UK is full of 'minipans', whose packaging is probably worth more than the instrument.) Bear in mind that a student with particular additional needs will attract additional funding which could be used to buy a piece of equipment that they need in order to play music meaningfully.

World music instruments

The world music instruments used most often in schools are generally quite 'low tech' and mostly percussion. It is relatively easy to make those initial sounds with them, but they can all lead to complex rhythms. This makes them eminently suitable for students with additional needs, and most suitable for true inclusion.

However, there is a certain amount of preciousness that comes with these instruments, especially if they are new into the UK education system. Tutors invite students to remove footwear to play gamelan, and steel pan enthusiasts roll their eyes at the thought of any notation. Of the instruments listed below, schools are unlikely to own their own gamelan, but there are charities and music services that hire them out (with a trained instructor, of course) and they are well worth the effort involved.

Tamboo bamboo are, as their name suggests, long bamboo poles. Their origin goes back to before steel pans in Trinidad and Tobago, where ex-slaves stamped them on the ground as they marched at Carnival. When the authorities banned them for sounding too threatening, the Trinidadians set about discovering what sounds they could make from old biscuit tins, dustbins and oil drums, and the rest is history (see 'Steel pans' below). In schools they are usually made of plastic. The firm marketing them in the UK trades as Bamboo Tamboo and does workshops on them, with helpful online resources.

The advantages of tamboo bamboo are that they are big, highly visual, very light and very instant. Students have to be on their feet (or in a wheelchair) in a circle, working now as a big team, then as a smaller section, playing increasingly more complex rhythms, or, if that is not possible, just maintaining a beat. There are no tricky hand or finger movements, so these would be suitable to use with all students with additional needs except perhaps some with **physical difficulties** and limited hand or arm movement. Tamboo bamboo is a great lead into tackling drums with more complicated techniques.

Dhols and *tablas* have become a common sight in our schools. From the South East Asian tradition, they are both percussion instruments. One is played with slender curved sticks, one with hands; dhols are usually worn around the neck, and players sit cross-legged on the floor to play tablas. They have a striking and very powerful sound all of their own. Usually they are taught by a visiting teacher from a local music service. If the rest of the class is playing a dhol, there should be no reason why any children with additional needs shouldn't join in. **Wheelchair users** can rest the instruments on their laps, those with limited arm movement need them placing within striking distance. **Children with VI** need introducing carefully to them.

Djembes and *samba*: Djembes originate in Africa and have been a familiar sight in the school music department for some time. Samba comes from Brazil with its origins in Africa. Like tamboo bamboo, you can play increasingly complex rhythms (or not) on them. For the pupils, especially the more challenging and attention-seeking ones, the possibility of loudness just jumps out at them; the drums are generally robust and can survive their enthusiasm.

One advantage of djembes is that you are seated to play them, and this brings all players down to the height of the wheelchair user. If keeping the bases off the ground is a problem for wheelchair users and other students with limited movement, specially designed stands are available. Samba is usually played standing, or even marching or dancing, but those unable to do this for any length of time can easily sit to play. It may be a problem that some djembes are made of animal skin. There may be students who are allergic to it (and vegans may indeed refuse to touch them). It is best to get ones with synthetic skins.

Gamelan: These gloriously visual instruments have something to offer children with all additional needs. There are two main types: Javanese and Balinese.

Basically they are pentatonic and consist of sets of metallophones and gongs; a full gamelan has two sets of tuning – pelag and slendro. UK schools generally buy the slendro, as pelag is not pentatonic. Each gamelan is individually hand-made and has its own tuning, which can make it difficult to play along with Western instruments (or even together with another gamelan!).

Gamelan suits just about every student with additional needs. Those with **PMLD** can sit between the gongs and experience the physicality of the sound; **wheelchair users** can put the pots on their knees or on the tray. **Students with autism** can go into their own world. This gives everyone a great freedom because the sounds always blend.

Students who are blind or visually impaired will enjoy the wonderful patterns made by the harmonics. Those who are **deaf or hearing impaired** will love the visual and physical nature of the instrument, and enjoy working in an ensemble. However, they may play the instruments too hard and knock them out of tune, and what little they can hear may be difficult to make sense of with so many harmonics being present.

Pupils who are on the **autistic spectrum** or who have **Asperger's syndrome** may enjoy the precise number patterns, based on a count of eight, which are traditionally needed to play the gamelan properly.

Figure 4.1 Blind children leading themselves into the gamelan.

The one group that the gamelan may not suit, unless in the hands of a behaviour management specialist, comprises **students with challenging behaviour**; they may be less willing to experiment with different cultures or completely different sounds. A gong in the wrong hands can ruin your day! Also some **children with autism** may be unable to cope without the Western tuning.

There are authenticity rules for gamelans, such as taking off footwear and also not stepping over any of the separate instruments. UK teachers divide between those who go with the rules and those who consider them unnecessarily 'precious'.

Guitars and ukuleles

For class guitar teaching, the traditional Spanish guitar is best. The nylon strings are gentler on beginners' fingertips, and the slightly wider necks are easier to fit your fingers onto, rather than the thinner jumbo steel string and twelve-string guitars. For those forming their own rock bands and studying with peripatetic tutors, the school will need some electric guitars, including at least one bass guitar. Always be sure to string at least one guitar for left-handed users. Guitars should always have cases, preferably hard ones. This will help to keep them in tune as well as protect them from damage.

The guitar, like the drum kit, in some but not all areas, can be perceived to be 'cool', and this is motivating for **students with learning and behaviour difficulties**. With carefully planned introductory lessons, using single-finger chords and well-known pop songs, pupils can be very successful.

Beginners on electric guitars can sound awful and they make a lot of noise – very satisfying for the players and highly irritating to the rest of the class. Use amps and headphones, and only allow pupils to have the jack leads when they have something to perform to the rest of the class. **Pupils with challenging behaviour** may be quite able, with naturally good fine motor skills; they may take quite easily to playing melody lines on guitar.

With open tuning, **pupils with Down's syndrome, MLD and SLD** can all make meaningful sounds, though variable progress, on a guitar.

Many pupils with **physical difficulties** – e.g. **those with cerebral palsy** – like the feel of the sound of an acoustic guitar. This can be made possible by placing the instruments flat on their wheelchair table or other surface. The pupil can then strum the strings while someone else changes the chords. Or the teacher could use open tuning and share the chords out between several pupils. If it is the sound of the strings that is the 'turn-on', then the somewhat unfashionable autoharp might be a good idea here. It is much easier for the helper to change chords on an autoharp than on a guitar.

For **pupils who are deaf and hearing impaired** the guitar has plus and minus features. The acoustic guitar can be felt rather than heard, but for those with some (limited) hearing an electric guitar may be better. Each pupil would be best with their own amp near to them (with headphones) so they can clearly detect what they are playing. An electro acoustic would seem to be the best of both worlds.

Guitars are ideal for **pupils who are visually impaired**. Because they hold the instrument to themselves, once they have learned the basics, they will instantly know where everything is, and they don't have to rely upon anyone else to set the equipment up. Any hardening of the fingertips should not affect the player's ability to read Braille, as this is read further down the finger on the pads just below the tips.

For **pupils with multi-sensory impairment** the teacher and support staff should experiment to see how well they would get on with a guitar.

Pupils who are autistic or have Asperger's syndrome may well take to the guitar, enjoying the sense of patterns and structure which playing chords and tunes on the guitar gives. Some with sensitive hearing may prefer the quieter sound of the acoustic guitar.

Students with learning difficulties can strum across the strings while a buddy (or a guitar teacher) holds down the chords or can have guitars tuned to one chord each.

Bass guitar is really easy to start playing. You only play one note at a time, and you can get through a few tunes playing only open strings (as they are tuned E, A, D, G). I taught a boy some of whose fingers were fused together. His friends had formed a rock band, and he was easily able to join in as their bass player.

Although the principle is the same, *ukuleles* are much easier to play and learn than guitars. Having only four strings, there are fewer notes to hold down with the fingerboard hand. A word of warning: there are cheap ukuleles which go out of tune overnight and there are those that hold their tuning for weeks and months. One chord songs are ideal of course, such as 'Frère Jacques' and 'It's Raining It's Pouring', or you can use two-chord songs by splitting the students into two groups, one playing on one chord and one on the other.

Steel pans

Steel pans (originally known as steel drums), like tamboo bamboo, originated in Trinidad and Tobago and, as mentioned above, grew out of experimenting with sounds from different metal containers. In the end, the best quality metal came from old oil drums. For a while, pan-tuners experimented with purpose made drums, but they were no better and cost more than a second-hand oil drum.

As different musicians all over Trinidad were experimenting with the possible sounds, and real notes, they ended up with a plethora of different layouts which endure to this day and make it quite difficult for teachers and students alike until you get your head exactly around how you are going to manage this situation.

They did, however, standardise quite a few of the pans around the end of the twentieth century, renaming the tenor pan soprano pan (which more accurately conveys its true range). Pans do correspond to SATB, and Table 4.1 demonstrates which pan does what.

Table 4.1 Naming of steel pans

Pitch	Pan	Number of individual ↓ drums	Usually plays
S Soprano	Soprano – low D [aka D tenor]	1	Melody
	Soprano – low C [aka C tenor]	1	
	Double tenor	1	
A Alto	Single second	1	High chord, counter melody
	Oversize single second	1	
	Double second	2	
	Quadraphonics	4	
T Tenor	Single guitar	1	Low chords
	Double guitar	2	
	Cello	3	
	Four cello	4	
B Bass	Single bass	1	Bass line
	Double bass	2	
	Triple bass	3	
	Tenor bass	4	
	Low six bass	6	
	Low nine bass	9	
	Twelve bass	12	

*Less used in **bold italics***

All pans have historical reasons for their names, but these names can confuse, and they can shut out would-be players and teachers.

Pans are either painted or chromed (for extra protection and looks). The higher the pitch, the more likely it is to be chromed.

Steel pans are individually hand-made. In the UK we mostly buy from the UK (usually London) and Trinidad. There are some prolific pan-makers in Switzerland, Finland and Germany.

Strenuous international efforts have been made to standardise the layouts of all pans. So far most new sopranos are circles of fifths, each drum of the triple cello is a diminished chord, each drum of the tenor bass is an augmented chord, and the notes of the low six bass, if positioned correctly, lead round as whole tone scales.

The beauty of steel pans is their inclusiveness. Some pans have a two octave span of increasingly smaller-sized, higher-pitched notes. This provides a suitable challenge for the very able, including **children with Asperger's or on the autistic spectrum**; single basses can have just five notes, and guitar pans nine notes, each with a huge surface area ideal for students with limited arm movement, or for students who can only play slowly (and **students with moderate learning difficulties**). And friends of different musical ability can work meaningfully together in the same ensemble.

Their disadvantage is their size and their not so obvious vulnerability. They are made individually by hand, can be knocked out of tune, and tuners in the UK are few and far between. New-build schools tend not to be creating music rooms big enough for pans to be kept in and to be kept standing. There are various solutions to this, the easiest one being buying singles rather than doubles and tenor or double basses rather than big six basses.

Although a steel pan is and can be an individual instrument, it is as a whole band/class that it is best learned and played. Students need each other to create this satisfying sound, so they soon realise that it is in their own interest to co-operate with others.

One great advantage that steel pans have over just about every other instrument is that they are free-standing. Pupils stand to play them and do not need to lose their independence or freedom of action by having to hold or support the instrument. Thus the pan in no way threatens or compromises the pupil's security or dignity. (There are already professional **wheelchair using** steel pan players who use specially adapted pan stands that clip on to the wheelchair.)

Deaf and hearing impaired pupils would feel vibrations from the big bass pans if both the pans and they themselves were standing on resonant boards, but you do need to be careful that they don't knock the notes out of tune. For **pupils who are blind or visually impaired**, steel pans should present very few problems as long as the pupil plays the same individual instrument each time (being hand-made, there are always slight variations).

Give **pupils on the autistic spectrum** opportunities to experiment on the steel pans individually before they are expected to work as part of a group.

Other world instruments, such as anklungs, singing bowls, autoharps, marimbas, sitars and taiko drums, are occasionally found in mainstream music departments, and they can be of some use for individual students, but we wouldn't recommend that you invest in a set. Local music services, university music departments and charities sometimes offer lessons on the bigger instruments, and these are offers worth taking up.

Steel pans were placed in schools all over the UK in the late seventies and early eighties as a response to Section Eleven of a government act. This offered grants to any school or institution that came up with a good idea to combat racism and promote multi-culturalism. At all-white Foxwood School in a deprived area of Leeds, head teacher Bob Spooner bought a set of steel pans. I was an English teacher there at the time, but with a history of anti-racist activities; the music teacher didn't like the pans, so Mr Spooner asked me to meet the new peripatetic teacher, StClair Morris, and help him teach them. I went to have a look at them. It was love at first sight. And soon after meeting these beauties, we got our steel band going; I became the music teacher, then Head of Music, then Head of Expressive Arts, but even sooner I forgot that the pans were 'a positive example of black culture'. It became irrelevant as I realised 1. what a lovely sound they could make, and 2. just how truly inclusive they were.

Victoria

Orchestral instruments

All pupils need to be given the opportunity to try to play the different orchestral instruments as well as to hear them. Short projects which introduce these instruments may discover hidden unexpected abilities. Teachers should be careful that all students observe basic hygiene rules and do not exchange mouthpieces when playing woodwind and brass instruments.

As we have written elsewhere, students with **behavioural difficulties** are often underachieving potential high fliers and may well succeed on the orchestral instrument of their choice. Teachers need to be patient and flexible and allow students to try things out in their own time.

Pupils with physical difficulties (including PMLD) should not be denied the pleasure of attempting to play these instruments. The physical difficulties will determine which instruments should be attempted.

There was one boy whose family thought he was frightened of musical instruments because he screamed whenever he saw them. One day the classroom assistant gave him a violin bow to hold, and together they stroked the instrument's strings. The boy stopped screaming and started smiling. It was not fear, his family realised, but frustration at not being able to touch and play the desired object.

Pupils who are deaf or hearing impaired will enjoy the vibro-tactile experience of the orchestral instruments, especially the low-pitched strings: cellos and double basses.

> The local string trio were visiting a school. The cellist was slightly alarmed when a deaf boy with SLD threw himself at her feet and lay on the floor before her, but she kept her nerve and went on playing, and as she did, the boy began taking in the vibrations and kicking the floor in time with the music.

Students with MLD, in our experience, are able to make sounds very quickly on brass instruments. It sounds good when all play single notes to fit with others, although further progression can be difficult.

Pupils who are blind or visually impaired will be able to learn any instrument they choose. As this is an area in which they are very likely to succeed, these pupils should be at the front of the queue if there are limited places for tasters. (See Sally Zimmerman's book published in 1998 by RNIB.)

Classroom and miscellaneous instruments

The voice is the most natural musical tool/instrument, yet it renders the user most vulnerable. The recent upsurge in interest in pop singing and the many television competitions for singers have enthused unprecedented numbers of pupils. The *microphone* brings power effortlessly to the voice as volume, and, of course, with volume comes personal power. (The website Sing Up has available a comprehensive set of resources of songs, ideas and activities that suit children with all different additional needs.)

For **pupils with challenging behaviour or MLD** the microphone offers power and street cred. I have seen a music teacher in Leeds take a class of pupils, mostly girls with no self-esteem and absolutely no social graces, and have them as putty in his hands as they queued up to take their turn with karaoke. And later that term these very same pupils took solo spots in an evening production of *Grease*.

In one school, pupils, including some with **Down's syndrome**, always finish their music lessons off with a karaoke type performance, taking turns to hold a microphone and sing along with their favourite pop song.

Pupils with **dyslexia, dyscalculia and dyspraxia**, as long as they do not feel uncomfortable about their voice, will be liberated by singing and can achieve well.

With an effects unit, **pupils with physical difficulties** can create satisfying and imaginative musical sounds and can experiment with the sounds that their own voices create.

Pupils who are hearing impaired should be empowered by the amplified sound of their own voice. Microphones will not be effective with the profoundly deaf unless they can feel the vibrations of the amplifier, and this is best achieved by both pupil and amplifier standing on a sounding board (or nicely resonant wooden floor). These pupils may enjoy being in a signing choir.

For pupils who stammer or who have **Tourette's syndrome** singing can be truly liberating, as it usually transcends the difficulties they encounter in speech.

Drum kits (including electronic kits and drum pads)

It is a good idea to have at least three drum kits if possible, with one permanently set up for left-handed players. One set should always be ready for the drummers to play along with the school's band, be it rock, jazz or steel.

Daniel was a pupil whose father was a professional drummer, and whose intended high school had closed before he was old enough to go to it. Consequently he lived miles from anyone else in his class and wasn't particularly happy at school. His one consolation was his drum kit lessons with the 'world's greatest drum kit "peri"'. Everybody expected him to follow in his father's footsteps and be a professional musician. One day the head teacher called him out of lessons at a moment's notice to stand in for the rock band's regular drummer who was ill. The local MP was paying a visit, with the photographers in tow. Alas, the regular drummer was right-handed. Daniel was not. Daniel was just about to swap the snare and the hi-hat over when the head stopped him. 'No time for that,' he called. 'Just play.' The following discussion between head and pupil cannot be recorded here. Daniel spent three days at home. The episode ended in no more drum kit lessons and no musical career.

For pupils with MLD and/or challenging behaviour the drum kit is often *the* instrument. It has associations of power, and of masculinity, and it has great street cred. Often boys resent girls being good at the drum kit, and they try to 'psych them out' of playing well. In our experience, girls with emotional problems often love learning to play the drum kit and will totally discard their poor behaviour long enough to learn this instrument. Boys, however, may need carefully planned five to ten minute learning bursts or it can be quite counter-productive, as they vent their frustration at their very quickly realised incompetence on the drums.

For pupils with PMLD, cerebral palsy and other physical difficulties staff should arrange and adjust the various pieces of the drum kit to enable pupils to play.

For pupils who are deaf or hearing impaired drum kits, and in fact all other drums, have the vibro-tactile element. They can develop and improve their sense of rhythm through copying. Pupils get feedback from the feeling of the vibrations and also visually, especially if they are working with a partner who is on another kit.

For pupils who are visually impaired staff should approach drum kits with great care. They can be instantly very loud, and unless the pupil is forewarned, the noise can be terrifying.

For pupils with autism and Asperger's syndrome it is hard to generalise about the drum kit. They may be intrigued by the patterns that can be created by the way that they are played or by the way the kit is set up. When pupils develop a liking for drums, they may become obsessive about them – it will be important to ensure that they understand about having to take turns.

Glockenspiels, xylophones and chime bars

If your vision of chime bars consists of an assortment of blue plastic rolls with rotting rubber and rusty pins, put it to one side and get out the 'Percussion Plus' catalogue. The catalogue includes a range of robust, 'childproof' instruments that allow pupils to enjoy playing without being anxious about breakages. For preference, choose alto-pitched instruments.

For students with learning difficulties chime bars allow them to physically move pitch around and experiment with it. **Pupils with Down's syndrome** and similar learning difficulties need only be given their own note, and they will always make a satisfying contribution to the pieces played as ensembles. Pupils with limited motor skills can have just the one note to look for and concentrate on. Over time, and when they are ready, each pupil can be given more notes.

The best glockenspiels are those that look like regular keyboards with white naturals and black sharps and flats, and have notes the same size as piano keys. For **pupils with SLD** there is a one octave diatonic glockenspiel (C–C with only white notes).

For **students with physical difficulties** chime bars come in various sizes and can easily be positioned so that pupils with little control over their movements can get to them. It is also possible to attach a beater to the wrist of a pupil who finds it hard to grip.

Pupils who are deaf or hearing impaired can enjoy playing chime bars even though the sound may need to be felt rather than heard. Wooden tone bars are specially designed for pitch work with deaf pupils. The sound can be felt by touching the sides, is easier to hear and dies away quickly (thus avoiding the confusion of sounds building up); they have less harmonic confusion than instruments with metal sounds.

Chime bars and tone bars are particularly suitable for **pupils with visual impairments**; they are held securely in the hand and can be used independently in ensemble playing.

For **students with moderate-to-severe learning difficulties** removable glockenspiel notes can be a nightmare and are only advisable if the teacher desperately likes the flexibility. Far better to have chime bars if you need to hand out fewer notes.

Keyboards (and the piano)

There are multitudes of types of electronic keyboards out there in the shops and, unfortunately, even more lying around in our schools. Their best features are also their worst features: endless switches and dials that prevent a person from playing a melody or constructing a chord or keeping time for themselves. What a head of music would buy if they were starting from scratch, and if money were no object, would probably be different from the reality. And the reality is, too often, the worst possible scenario: lots of different types of keyboards, some not working or missing keys; headphones broken, or working in only one ear. (Fortunately there are firms which specialise in return-of-post headphone repairs, and they can transform the music teacher's life.)

Pupils with learning difficulties enjoy and benefit from experimenting with the sounds made by a keyboard. For these pupils, marking note names, scales or chords with letters or colours is probably necessary. Playing pentatonic tunes on just the black notes is a good way to give these pupils a sense of achievement. For some learners there are just too many notes: try putting blocks on either side of an octave or two to limit the choice. Colour-coding of chords works well on keyboards. (See website for resource: www.routledge. com/9781138231849.)

If the teacher systematically insists on the whole class using headphones, and keeps a wary eye on the **pupils with attention and behaviour problems**, then keyboards can be the way through to these pupils working, learning and playing for its own sake. With no one to show off to, no one to disrupt, they will eventually get bored of listening to the pre-set tunes and start to teach themselves. With headphone splitters the teacher can quickly reward those who are working well and give them little bursts of attention. Splitters, again, are good for getting these pupils to co-operate and work in pairs.

Surprisingly, touch sensitivity can spoil the performance for pupils with poor motor skills, and this may irritate pupils who also have emotional problems. (It is best to buy keyboards that can turn this facility on and off.) Everybody loves all the things that the keyboards can do. With all the latest technical developments there should be enough to challenge and absorb all pupils, including those with behaviour difficulties.

If there is a real piano in the room, pupils with behaviour problems will often gravitate towards it. They may say that they really like the sound better, and this may be true, but the pupil cannot control the volume or use headphones and so other pupils will be distracted. The piano should be for the teacher's use only in general music lessons. Pupils who are taking piano lessons can use it at pre-arranged times. In order to check out a pupil's genuine interest in a piano, you could let them use the one in the empty practice room (if you have one) and see if they stay as long on that as they do on the one in the main teaching room.

For pupils with cerebral palsy you can get key guards and switch guards. These are fitted over the keyboard to enable a pupil with poor muscle tone to avoid playing unwanted notes and rhythms. Note clusters are easier to play than individual notes. There are many good programs to use for **pupils with CP** if they want to record a keyboard piece.

Some pupils with CP may have good foot control – placing the keyboard on the floor and taking off the pupil's shoes and socks can be amazingly liberating for the pupil and enable them to join in real time in an ensemble piece.

For many **pupils with Asperger's syndrome/autism** there is something about the keyboard (including piano and organ) which fascinates. This does not apply to all, but if they are interested, then they can be obsessive, which can become a problem when it comes to finishing a session. They may wish to audition all the sounds within the keyboard and may well have certain playing routines which they do each time they play – these may be more about the patterns created than about the sound. **Some pupils with ASD** may find wearing headphones a frightening or uncomfortable experience. Allow the student to hold the headphones first and put them on for themselves when they feel comfortable with the idea.

Pupils with severe autism often put their hands over their ears when any music is played. This may not be because it is too loud – it may just be that the sound was unexpected and they are giving themselves time to come to terms with it. Do not be put off by the hands over the ears – or even adverse reactions. With careful management the pupil may learn to get used to new sounds and may actually enjoy them in time. There may be some pupils who are truly sensitive to all or some particular sounds; work with the TAs to establish what these are.

Pupils on the autistic spectrum often love the pure acoustic sounds of a real piano. Where students seem to be locked away in their own worlds, music can be the interface that makes the breakthrough, and instruments with pure acoustic sounds are more likely to help them do it. There may also be something about the precise (chromatic) layout of the notes that may make a piano lend itself to being easily mastered and understood/enjoyed by the pupil with autism. Some love the repeated patterns that the keyboard provides and will relish the endless possibilities, going on to play tunes in many different keys. Others may find a pattern they enjoy, repeating it over and over again, and not moving on.

There is very little vibration for a **profoundly deaf pupil** to feel with keyboards. If they are connected to an amp and the speakers are placed near to the pupil, preferably in a room with a resonant floor or on a sounding board, then some use may be made of them. Pupils with some hearing may be able to turn them up enough to benefit from them. A grand piano is probably the best solution for pupils who are deaf. If they can be around the piano actually touching the wood, then they will get a real feeling for the sound. A wooden floor will make this even better, with the vibrations being felt through the feet.

In his later and deafer years Beethoven, whenever he was at the piano playing or composing, would hold a piece of wood in his mouth which led down onto the soundboard, and in this way he could feel what he was playing.

Pupils who are hearing impaired do manage to learn to play the piano sometimes to a very high level, e.g. pianist Julia Shirabe from Japan. She gained a degree in music, as did Paul Whittaker (specialising on the organ), now with Music and the Deaf.

Blind students and those with VI are often fully at home on a piano. (The teacher should be careful not to go overboard on the compliments when they outperform the others!) They will find playing a conventional piano better than keyboards because of the vibratory feedback felt through the fingers.

For **pupils with PMLD** developing the hand control to press down a group of notes on the keyboard may be a huge achievement.

Hand percussion

Hand percussion can produce wonderful sounds. Alas, it is just all too easy to hand round a mixed box of maracas, tambourines, wood blocks and piercingly loud cowbells and let carnage ensue. We recommend that if you do hand the box round, then get hold of Johnny Dean's *Latin Percussion* and spend some time looking at ways of producing the most interesting sounds and rhythms, except of course when you are improvising! Also we recommend that everyone has the same instrument at any one time, so that they can hear the contrasts and different timbres between say wood blocks and maracas. A pupil's particular needs are not going to affect greatly their choice of small percussion instrument. Everybody loves the Claterpillar and you don't have to be on the autistic spectrum to adore how it moves, how it sounds and how it feels.

Technology

Technology has opened the world of performing, composing and improvising, especially for **pupils with PD and with PMLD**: at its simplest level it enables students to deliberately cause a sound to be made, and at the most advanced it enables them to play alongside mainstream musicians in the Paralympic orchestra. The key to musical success for students with physical difficulties is finding the correct interface between their bodies and the technology. This is usually done through switches, which are pressed by whichever is the most appropriate or movable part of the body. One can also put the body and/or the wheelchair through a soundbeam. With the tap of a finger or the nod of a head a student enters the world of 'everything is musically possible', releasing sounds that have been created for them – single notes, chords or just sounds.

For **students with physical difficulties** the *soundbeam* (originally developed for dancers, then taken up as a therapeutic tool) has been recognised as having enormous potential in the music classroom. This is a touch free device which uses sensor technology to translate body movement into music and sound. This could be any musical instrument sound or sound effect and pupils can 'play' an instrument merely by moving a hand or foot. Key issues such as timing, pitch and rhythm are just as important to a soundbeam player as to any instrumentalist, and skills of concentration are essential when playing as part of a group.

Using feet is a good way for some pupils to operate a mixing desk. I have seen a young man with **cerebral palsy** run the mixing desk for a whole show with all the equipment spread out along the floor, i.e. professional mixing desk, computer running Cubase and keyboard. His wheelchair enabled him to move along from one piece of equipment to another (details are available from the Drake Music Project).

The music teacher can use the pupil's personal switch to connect up to various pieces of ICT equipment in order for them to create meaningful musical sounds. There are various pieces of equipment on the market which allow this.

Pupils with ASD or Asperger's syndrome are often skilled and enthusiastic users of computers but may also be obsessive about their use. If other pupils are using computers in the music lesson, the student with ASD may find it difficult to concentrate on anything else. Plan separate music technology lessons for classes that include pupils with ASD so that they are able to develop both the practical and the technological skills of music.

Anita is deaf and uses British Sign Language to communicate. She also has multiple physical disabilities, learning and communication disabilities. Our one-to-one music sessions are based on principles of musical and intensive interaction.

I bring a variety of instruments to our sessions. Anita always begins with the iPad. She chooses her favourite program – a house music grid-based program. She taps on a coloured square and sees it pulse with light as the music thumps a grinding bass riff. She doesn't hear the riff, but she can feel it through her mini Bluetooth speaker which she holds in her hand. She systematically switches colours (which are different riffs) on and off in rainbow order, then switches them on in combination and invites me and her carer/BSL interpreter to join in. She likes it when we dance along and then have to stop suddenly when she turns off the speaker. The lights are still pulsing but she can feel the sound has stopped.

Anita also likes feeling the vibrations of acoustic instruments. She plays short sounds on each and enjoys strumming the snares on the snare drum as though they were banjo strings. She also enjoys the feel of the keys on a piano and accordion. She doesn't play to a particular beat, but she repeats ways of playing that feel good, making her own rhythms.

Joanna

For **students with VI**, programs with voice-over enable them to navigate the screen, and many become adept at the most complicated of programs. For **those with HI,** programs which represent music visually will give them an idea of how music works, especially if the computer is connected to amps and to resonance boards which will allow the students to feel the vibrations.

Archie, aged 9 and on the autistic spectrum, attended our music sessions, but he would always sit on his own in a corner, playing on his iPad or the computer. He gave the impression that playing glockenspiels was beneath him and wasn't a keen singer. One lesson I sat with him and asked him to show me on the computer what music he liked. This was electronic dance music, so I downloaded 'Garage Band' on an iPad for him to try. It could only have taken a couple of weeks and he was off! Not only was he now being musical in music lessons, but he was composing at home as well.

Chloe

iPads

For a long time now touch screens have enabled people with physical and/ or communication difficulties to communicate. This technology is now refined and available to everyone via iPads/tablets, phones and touch screen computers. These are liberating for everyone but especially people with limited movement or language.

iPads work well connected up to workstations with headphones where each pupil can choose their own sounds or loops to compose music using such programs as 'Garage Band'. This is excellent for individual working and can also work with a group. Each iPad can be set up as an instrument to form a band. All students can thus play through a central mixing desk and the group can jam, or perform together in any style of music or with whatever instruments they choose. This frees up the musical imagination without the technical restrictions imposed by learning the acoustic instrument itself. However, going through one central control does mean it is not easy to identify the individual student's contribution to the ensemble. It may be best to use separate amps, at least for public performances.

There is no limit to the sounds available via the app store and many apps are free at a basic level. See 'iPad music teacher' pages for online discussions of the best materials (https://ipadmusiced.wordpress.com/).

Conclusion

Choosing an instrument for a young person with special/additional needs is broadly the same as choosing one for anyone else. Some students will want to fit in with the rest of the class; some will want to do their own thing. The ones who want to fit in will most likely be the ones whose additional needs make them feel isolated, and they may, of course, choose an instrument that does not suit their abilities. Then the teacher must use their judgement about what is more important: the musical nature of a music session or the pupil's social reason for playing any given instrument.

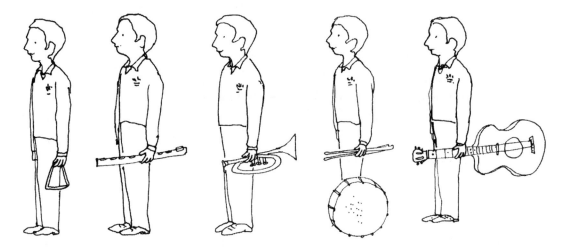

Figure 4.2 Actually Colin wanted to play them all!

5 Listening, improvising, performing and composing

Listening, improvising, performing and composing are really all that music in school is about. The National Curriculum states that in KS3:

> Pupils should build on their previous knowledge and skills through performing, composing and listening.

> Pupils should be taught to:

> - play and perform confidently in a range of solo and ensemble contexts using their voice, playing instruments musically, fluently and with accuracy and expression
> - improvise and compose; and extend and develop musical ideas by drawing on a range of musical structures, styles, genres and traditions
> - use staff and other relevant notations appropriately and accurately in a range of musical styles, genres and traditions
> - identify and use the inter-related dimensions of music expressively and with increasing sophistication, including use of tonalities, different types of scales and other musical devices
> - listen with increasing discrimination to a wide range of music from great composers and musicians
> - develop a deepening understanding of the music that they perform and to which they listen, and its history.

In this chapter we consider how pupils with additional needs might respond to various approaches and be supported in these different aspects of music lessons.

Listening

Music is everywhere. Casually, every day we listen to music: doing our homework, doing the housework, sitting on buses, sitting in trains, walking down the street – buried in our own sound, blocking out the other sounds. We dance to it,

Box 5.1 Our listening scheme (Jaquiss and Philips 1992)

Working in an underprivileged area of Leeds in the 1990s, Pablo and I spent quite a few sessions together writing our music course for KS3 and for GCSE Music. We felt very strongly that our students needed:

1. some sort of familiarity with major classical composers from all the main musical periods; awareness of the composers' names, their most famous pieces of music, what countries and centuries they came from and the instrumentation of said pieces (and for GCSE, some more besides, of course);
2. to understand different genres of music and what types of music, with which instruments, came from which parts of the world;
3. to recognise tunes that they heard on newly emerging video games, in films, advertisements and television programmes;
4. their own taste in music recognised, celebrated and seen for what it has in common with all other musical genres, and this to be done in a factual, not sycophantic, way.

Neither Pablo nor I were music specialists as far as teacher-training goes. He was a mathematics teacher who played guitar and bass guitar in various local indie rock bands; I was a linguist and English and drama trained teacher who had been head of music for a few years and had recently been made head of expressive arts. I also played in various women's comic indie bands and ran my own school steel band.

Thus Pablo and I were, in some sense, amateurs, but most importantly had no baggage. We read the music curriculum with fresh eyes and were able to work out how we could make it work for our vulnerable, challenging, disadvantaged students. Recognising that some of our students were barely literate, while others were university material (or would have been if life wasn't getting in their way!), we devised a set of differentiated grids for them to fill in while listening to four very short pieces of music. They were in this order:

classical;
world;
theme tune/pop classic;
pop.

We used Beethoven's Fifth, the 'William Tell Overture', 'Für Elise', any classical piece we thought they might have heard before. We put up a grid on the board and as the music played, we filled in the information for them and with them. They were listening and they were writing, thus they were not talking. As the weeks passed, more and more was asked of them, such as clapping the beats, finding the first one, working out the time signature, but in the first place their input was to tick if they had heard it before, to put a smiley or sad face to say whether they liked it, and also to put an order of preference. To be allowed to say that they didn't like something was very important, but we treated it matter-of-factly and talked about different tastes.

We also linked each set of music to a musical topic, for example an element. If the element was dynamics, we would choose songs that were either very loud or very soft or included some very obvious crescendos etc. If the topic was the 'guitar', then we would demonstrate various genres of music that all used guitars. After that we might draw and label the various types of guitar and try playing one in the practical sessions.

Three of the best moments of my teaching life were connected to our listening scheme:

1. An Ofsted inspector told us it was the best system of introducing listening to music she had ever seen, and that we should publish it.
2. Richard (challenging behaviour but lovable) opened the music room door with the exclamation, 'Not bloody Handel again!' (I told him to watch his language, but I was bursting with pride that he recognised and remembered the music that I had played him two days before.)
3. Students in parallel classes started asking each other what the chart song was. We always played only the first two seconds of these at first listening and invited guesses. Pablo and I ended up using four current pop songs each week!

Table 5.1 Listening sheets

Listening Sheet 1

Name _____ Date _____

Title	Composer and nationality	Player/s and period or style	1	2	3

1. Heard it before   2. Beats to the bar   3. Order of preference

Listening Sheet 2

Name _____ Date _____

Title	Composer and nationality	Player/s and period or style	Instruments	1	2	3

1. Heard it before   2. Beats to the bar   3. Order of preference

Listening Sheet 3   Name _____   Date _____

Title	Composer and nationality	Player/s and period or style	Instrumentation	Tempo/dynamics	1	2	3

1. Heard it before   2. Beats to the bar   3. Order of preference

in our wheelchairs and on our feet. We walk down the aisle to it, bury our loved ones to it. We hear Prokofiev announce the arrival of Newcastle United, and Gerry and the Pacemakers bring on Liverpool. The makers of films, television and radio programmes and advertisements use music, newly composed or already existing, to announce beginnings and endings, and to set scenes and moods.

Some of us go out to gigs or concerts and just watch and listen, as we would a film. Music that someone else has composed and recorded forms a big part of our culture and every day experience. Pupils will form their friendships around a particular style of 'pop' music; they will form their musical tastes around their friendships. They will choose their clothes according to their musical preferences. And it is the same for children with additional needs. No one now is surprised to see someone in a wheelchair with pink hair, or a blind person with piercings.

Music is so much part of our everyday life, and yet everywhere we talk over it. We talk, shout even, over music in nightclubs and bars. Too often the music is a background to our lives, and this can make the listening part of the Music lesson quite difficult. And it can make taking a class to a town hall concert fraught with shushes.

Listening in class

Listening can be one of the hardest components of any Music course. Teachers are asking pupils to listen out for instruments that they rarely, if ever, hear or see, and to have an emotional response to classical music that may be well outside their normal experience. And they are being asked to 'be quiet'! For those used to talking over the television it can be very difficult. And to get pupils to listen critically, and with discernment, is quite another thing, hence its importance in the music curriculum. Teachers may find details of our listening scheme helpful; it incorporates a series of differentiated Listening Sheets which ask students to listen out for things such as tempo and dynamics, and to express their order of preference of the pieces played to them.

One teacher in a primary Special School decided to introduce some new songs from a particular style of music to her pupils. She played Tammy Wynnette. 'I know that,' said Simon. 'That's "Stand by Your Man".' 'That's right,' said the teacher. As she pressed PLAY for Kenny Rogers' 'Lucille', Simon sang along with the lyrics. Then, 'Well, Simon,' the teacher smiled, 'and who is this?' 'Dolly Parton, "DIVORCE"' was the correct reply.

It turned out that the minibus driver was a country and western fan, and that for the past six months Simon had been having a veritable history of music lesson as he was transported to and from school every day.

Listening for pupils with challenging behaviour

Listening as part of a music lesson is much the same for all learners, with all different types of special/additional needs. The students with challenging behaviour may be the first ones to 'kick off' when the class is asked to be quiet, but they could be articulating what the quieter children are thinking. What makes it difficult is getting pupils to put aside their other thoughts and their problems and lose themselves in listening to this other language that is music. If, ultimately, you are looking for pupils to just sit and enjoy/ appreciate some extended piece of music which is outside their normal experience, then the teacher has to start nearer home with familiar pieces of music such as those used on advertisements and computer programs and games.

One's aim, of course, must be listening in silence without talking at all, with concentration and an emotional response(!), but if you wait for total silence before the listening can start, then you may wait all lesson or even weeks.

> 'The Best of the Rest', a group of Leeds peripatetic teachers, was playing a concert at the local Special School for pupils with behavioural difficulties. Theirs was an eclectic group of instruments from crumhorns and ocarinas to steel pans and accordions. They played everything from folk music to film music to music from the charts. The time approached for the classical number. The pianist looked around nervously. 'Shall we miss the Scarlatti out?' she asked. 'No' was their reply.
>
> As she played, her eyes glued to the sheet music, a group of boys crept towards her, gazing lovingly at her fingers and the piano keyboard, holding their breath, and when she looked up at the end of the piece she found that she was not alone. The silence was so extreme – you could cut it with a knife.

Listening for pupils with severe and complex difficulties

Pupils with SLD and PMLD have short concentration spans, but they respond well to music, especially when staff understand the pupils' tastes. For some pupils listening is a multi-sensory experience: scarves are moved in time with the music, and the emotions in the music are picked up as textures felt through materials such as sandpaper and velvet to define the different types of sounds.

> We were listening to a piece of music in E minor by Evelyn Glennie. We gave the pupils chime bars and bell plates to form an E minor 7th chord. As the music progressed, they joined in following the lead of the music – quiet and slightly a-rhythmic. The listening was intense and the group gradually played on as the music was faded out.

Listening for pupils with physical difficulties

A pupil whose ability to go anywhere depends on other people may well have spent much time listening to music in transit. If they have had little access to switches and iPads which enable them to control their environment, they may have listened to other people's music and developed specific tastes, which are different from those of their peers.

There may be adjustments needed during/after the listening session for pupils with physical difficulties. Some may make notes on their laptops; others may need a discussion with their TA about what they have just heard (perhaps using switches). It's important to establish that the pupil and support worker should not talk during the musical excerpts. The TA should ensure that the pupil in a wheelchair is comfortable enough to sit still for the duration.

Listening for pupils with sensory impairment

A British Sign Language teacher was discussing the education of deaf and hearing impaired pupils with a high school music teacher: 'Do you teach music to the deaf?' he signed. 'Of course,' the teacher said. 'I wouldn't want anyone excluded from my lessons.' 'What's the point?' he shrugged and signed.

Even with 95 per cent hearing loss, the pupils with hearing impairment will get a lot of pleasure from listening. These pupils need to be near the speakers, on a resonant floor and/or with their own amplifier-receivers. Having videos of orchestras and bands may help, although the totally deaf may get nothing from them. Live acoustic instrumental music can be more accessible for these pupils than CDs. Visual displays on an interactive whiteboard with computer generated patterns can help. Many pupils now have cochlea implants, which makes listening to music so much more rewarding.

The teacher may invite pupils to clap different beats with some pieces of music. In that case, the pupils with HI will enjoy the social interaction of clapping along with the rest of the class. Do not be afraid to ask whether or not they can hear and what they can hear.

Pupils who are blind or VI live in a world of sound. They may enjoy a large and varied listening repertoire at an early age. The teacher must be sensitive to their extra knowledge. Listening, as a school activity, will increase their understanding of the music that they are already familiar with. Ensure that there are no extraneous noises which would distract the blind pupils but which normally don't bother other people. These might include the noise of the central heating or the buzz of a poorly recorded piece of music.

To read and make notes the blind pupils will have Braille and/or Screenwriter, and those with VI may prefer extra large print.

Listening for pupils with ASD

Sitting in a group of peers who are being quiet, listening and concentrating on the music will benefit the pupils on the autistic spectrum. It is good for them as a social activity. For a few of them it will be a marvellous voyage of discovery as they finally find the type of music that they really adore. Be aware, however, that pupils with autism may find it hard to sit for any length of time; be selective and extend listening periods gradually. Some pupils will enjoy listening to their own choice of music on an iPad with headphones, and this may be a way in to getting them to listen to other genres. They can be obsessive about certain pieces, however, and may need steering away from them. Listening should be a calming experience, but a TA should assess how the session is going and have an alternative activity ready if appropriate.

Listening to live music

Of course there is nothing like a live concert for everybody, with or without SEND. This is a truly multi-sensory experience as pupils see, hear and feel music. However, concerts must be geared to the age group of the pupils attending. If this is a local music service prom, the teacher should find out about the repertoire; if it is a visiting group, the content and length should be negotiated.

A town hall prom was attended by 800 primary school children, who were there to listen to, watch and be motivated and moved by the city's finest young players. The orchestra played first, an unfamiliar classical piece. Most of the audience was sighted and they were being treated to a veritable feast: double basses, harps, a tuba, the timpani, loads of wonderful orchestral instruments, some of them too big these days to fit into a school classroom. Those who were blind were having a similar aural experience. Next to play was the rock band, and after one number

(Continued)

the band leader invited the audience to clap along. It became a jolly and relaxed atmosphere; the children felt a part of the concert and were responding appropriately to a loud and amplified band. Unfortunately, when the next ensemble came on, the audience took it upon themselves to accompany them as well, and the clapping turned into not a joint experience but almost a competition in which the audience all but drowned out this acoustic set.

If you're doing listening properly, you are reaching into the students' own world, touching their own culture and leaving the comfort of your own knowledge and tastes behind. You will also of course be asking them to enter into the unfamiliar worlds of music they may have never heard before. You may be opening doors for pupils for whom so many doors are closed.

When you take them out to concerts or invite players in, you are supporting them as they become appreciative audiences of the future. They will clap at times for the wrong reasons (see above) and in the wrong places, and it is up to all the adults present to ensure that they enjoy live music without spoiling the enjoyment for other members of the audience or, of course, the players themselves. Concert performers depend on a live audience to give feedback, and they thrive on it, so getting the appreciation right is so very important all round.

The pupil could build up a 'listening, concert and musical activities' profile. This will be a good guide to their interests and abilities and can be used as a starting point for them to move off from. Listening in class should develop some awareness of other people's tastes.

Improvising

Perhaps the best starting point for performing or composing, or improvisation proper, is to explore instruments and find out what they can do, without instruction or restriction. Let your students hold them, tap them, shake them, scrape them together, pluck them. The 'Orff' approach encourages students to explore alternative ways of playing a given instrument before moving on (www.orff.org.uk).

Evelyn Glennie (an award-winning percussionist) tells of how, in her first week of learning drum kit, her percussion teacher gave her a stick to take home and find different ways of making sounds on and with it. Ms Glennie is also famously hearing-impaired which isn't really the point of this story.

The point is that she was given no instructions and had no one overseeing her first sounds. The following week she was given another part of the kit to experiment on. And so on. All students would benefit from this approach; children with additional needs would benefit doubly.

Improvising is good because there are no fixed rules. The teacher can set as few or as many boundaries as s/he wants. Pupils are liberated from the fear of playing the 'wrong' note, because there are no wrong notes, no wrong rhythms, no wrong combinations of instruments, no wrong switches. By listening to what they achieve accidentally, pupils will learn about their instruments and themselves musically, and then repeat anything that pleases them.

For children who can manipulate instruments easily with their hands untuned percussion is the usual starting place. For students with physical difficulties you will need switches, soundbeams, floor pads for stepping or rolling on.

For improvising with the voice, microphones with effects are liberating, as is making deliberately weird noises. We would describe all of this as musical 'scribble'. Teachers should be careful of voicing their opinion of the sounds made. It is not helpful to say that something sounds terrible; it is equally unhelpful to say 'That's great!' when it is just work in progress.

The beauty of working as a whole class on improvisation is that students are interacting with each other, listening to each other's sounds and responding to them. Without any instructions, they will be changing what they do in response to other sounds. And for the first time, perhaps, a student with additional needs will be fully participating in a class ensemble with their peers, with all the consequent social benefits.

To make the move from 'scribbling' to meaningful improvisation, we can use the usual pantheon of composition techniques: turn taking, outlining a basic structure, agreeing about stopping and starting, and using signs to demonstrate texture, dynamics and the like. It is a great introduction in general to the elements of music, and to working as an ensemble, and to listening.

Negotiate with pupils (and/or their TAs) the sorts of sign or symbol to use for 'stop' and 'go'. All instruments are fair game for improvising, but it is good to start with untuned percussion and observe how children handle these instruments. You then may choose whether to introduce a few rules as instruments get more delicate. Remember safe-guarding: avoid sharing wind instruments and students overtightening stringed instruments, or sitting under steel pans. You may start to put a structure on the music made, for example by following a poem or a story or asking pupils to musically illustrate a picture using some graphic notation they create.

A teacher may discover in an improvisation lesson that some students, particularly on the autistic spectrum, have natural musical ability that can only be discovered through free musical expression, and this musical ability may seem at odds with a student's academic ability.

Performing

Students arrive in your lessons with varying degrees of confidence. The teacher has a responsibility to set up a situation where all pupils feel comfortable and valued, where every note they sing and every note they play are valued. Performing here includes classroom practicals and public performance.

Why perform?

Pupils with special needs should be encouraged to perform for the same reason as anyone else:

- to improve concentration;
- to provide a sense of achievement – a 'buzz';
- to raise self-esteem;
- to provide opportunities for self-expression;
- to help them meet new challenges;
- to practise self-discipline;
- to receive recognition (as applause);
- to give a purpose to the learning.

In classroom performance you can afford to go wrong; on stage it's best not to. Classroom performance is more personal. Going on stage is also about all the extras, e.g. rehearsals, sense of audience, coping with nerves, appearance, choice of repertoire, etc. Many pupils with special educational needs take part meaningfully in public performances and can actually step outside their special needs status and take us all by surprise. Whereas a pupil with learning difficulties may have nothing to contribute to the school's chances of gaining the maths gold medal, they may well have something musical to offer which other people can appreciate, admire and enjoy.

Twenty years ago, after hearing a teenager in a choir singing like a nightingale in a local town hall Christmas concert, the local vicar asked why she wasn't taking up singing professionally. Her teacher invited him to have a chat with her, when he soon realised that, outside the singing world, she was a pupil with learning difficulties. Who knows what she could have achieved if she had been a teenager today – in a more inclusive setting?

I taught a boy with autism who would go to the piano and play an augmented chord every time he came into the music lesson. It was always the same augmented chord. His uncle, who always hated the sound, would beg me to teach his nephew 'Hot Cross Buns', but the boy wouldn't play it. The uncle did not understand the standard to which the pupil was actually working.

Another of my pupils, a boy with learning difficulties and poor motor skills, had to make an enormous effort to move his fingers from one note on the keyboard to the next. The day he played 'Hot Cross Buns' recognisably, and in time, we cheered. When his mother came to collect him, she said, 'Is that it?'

Ensembles and solos

Ensembles (from the French for 'together') provide excellent opportunities for pupils to work together, accommodating all the various types and standards of contribution. They can also be a comforting place to hide, safe in the knowledge that others will cover your own mistakes. However, some pupils with additional needs may never achieve successful ensemble playing, and solos will give them a better chance of musical success. Obviously both are important one particularly for working as a team and one for self-expression.

Performing for students with MLD

Many pupils with learning difficulties enjoy performing. It helps if the teacher can choose tunes that are already familiar and are rhythmically straightforward, and give careful consideration to the parts given to these students. Short pieces of music with lots of repetition are useful, and verses, lines or bars of music can be shared between pupils. However simple the part, the teacher should rehearse it seriously with pupils so that the contribution is meaningful. Performing on stage can mean a lot to pupils with learning difficulties; they will love it. This is the day they feel really good about themselves and it takes a special place in their memory.

For those who have perfect pitch or a sense of rhythm, performing provides a great opportunity, and they will gain in confidence as a result of doing something that they are demonstrably good at. Pupils with Down's syndrome, for example, are often enthusiastic singers whose performances bring pleasure to others, including families and classmates. Most pupils with MLD/SLD will be eager to take a meaningful part in school assemblies alongside their classmates. Working together as an ensemble means that the other students develop a greater understanding and tolerance of difference and diversity in school. This is good for everybody – but may take some time in establishing.

Karaoke-type events are popular and pupils often know all the words to songs (sometimes from the unlikeliest eras). For pupils with learning difficulties it is best to avoid songs with lots of complicated text and to teach them to sing 'la' when they forget the words. For solo performances or duets, choose a short piece that the pupils know very well. Always leave the audience wanting more – and not wishing there were less!

Performing for pupils with challenging behaviour

Attention-seeking pupils crave attention, whether it is praise/applause/ recognition for their achievements or being told off for ruining something. Being the one pupil, for example, who plays the last note (after everyone else has finished), or the one who disrupts someone else's performance, reliably gains them much-wanted attention. Performance is a time to harness and channel those needs. These pupils are often frustrated and clever and are likely to prove skilled performers; they could do well on stage, provided that they don't use it as an opportunity to gain the wrong type of attention. If you suspect that they are about to 'kick off' and spoil a performance for everyone, be firm and cut their act. If they don't turn their behaviour around this time, they will the next time.

Public performance is invaluable for the pupils with attention and behaviour problems. Besides all the things that performance is good for making you do, such as refining and improving your playing and giving a purpose to what may otherwise seem boring repetition, it can also make a difference to the pupils' emotional and social development. Such venues as care homes, nurseries and hospitals are good for pupils who are very self-centred. It gives them a chance to think about others, and select and extend their repertoire accordingly – learning nursery songs for younger children or old-time favourites for senior citizens. It can provide opportunities for them to attract the right sort of attention and earn praise for their efforts.

In the classroom it is important that pupils with challenging behaviour develop good routines. Unless the teacher is firm (and has turned all the keyboards off centrally), they will be the ones who move over to the instruments and start to play before they have listened to the instructions about what it is they have to do. (Always keep instructions as brief as possible to avoid this sort of problem.) They may try to take the best drum kit for themselves, or the most up-to-date keyboard etc., unless their equipment is clearly labelled and/or clear instructions are given at the start of the lesson. Prompts posted on the wall, such as 'Leave the drum kits set up as you find them', aren't really much use, except in retrospect, when you point to the remains of said kit and ask the offender, 'Didn't you see the notice!?'

It can be a good idea to let these pupils have trial sessions with the peripatetic teacher where they can get some more individualised tuition. However, it is sensible to send them with at least one other person, and never put the peripatetic in the position of being in a one-to-one with a pupil with behaviour problems.

Patronising and inaccurate praise will only confirm for them that adults are not serious, do not tell the truth, and can actually underestimate their pupils. It is important to be sincere at all times and develop ways of giving positive feedback even when the performance is less than brilliant: 'I can see that was a difficult piece for you, Jack, but well done for giving it a go.'

Performing for pupils with physical difficulties

Start by finding out what pupils can do for themselves. Playing in real time is a problem for some: their ears will tell them what they want to hear, their eyes will tell them where to go, but their hands just won't do it. However, there isn't much point in holding the pupil's hand in order that they can grip the beater and bang the chime, because then they are not controlling the sound. Consider getting them to operate instruments and equipment with other parts of their body, if they don't get far with their hands. They may need switches, soundbeams or iPads/tablets (see Chapter 4 on instruments).

At one school which prided itself on entering pupils with all sorts of SEND for the music exam, the support assistant and the peripatetic SEND music specialist were putting together the portfolio of recordings for Anastasia, a Year 11 girl with cerebral palsy. Despite the extra difficulties that Anastasia encountered, with help from the various teachers and support staff she was in with a chance of a GCSE grade C. But when it came to thinking about who was going to realise the composition and sing it for her, the girl begged the staff not to have her record her own song because, as she said herself, 'Even I can't tell what words I've sung.'

When putting pupils with physical difficulties on the stage, the teacher must ensure that the pupils feel comfortable about their position, and that their

Figure 5.1 When pupils with physical difficulties go on stage, make sure they are comfortable with their position and that their contribution is meaningful.

contribution is meaningful. In class they can try out how they fit into the ensemble, and they may legitimately decide against doing it in public. Physical access to and within public spaces (wherever possible) is now a right for everyone – so plan ahead with staff at concert halls etc. to be prepared for installing movable ramps, borrowing a hoist, etc. for the performance day.

There are some easy steps to successfully including students with physical difficulties in performance:

- using switches – improvising over other's playing;
- operating equipment with parts of the body over which they have perfect control, e.g. feet or head;
- computers using step time to input the sounds, then playing back in time;
- making atmospheric sounds not needing precise rhythms etc. (e.g. ocean drum, not wood block), keyboards with atmospheric sounds;
- paired work with mainstream pupils, or pupils with complementary strengths and needs;
- wheelchair dancing;
- short extracts, limited number of notes, large instruments;
- the pupil acting as composer.

Performing for pupils with sensory impairment

In order to perform accurately, pupils with hearing impairment will need good visual clues and may also need to watch their hands while they play. These pupils will benefit from lots of rhythm work using drums and hand-held percussion. To stay in time they can either feel the vibrations through the floor (or through a sounding board) and/or watch others for visual clues. They will respond well to graphic notation and visual directions. Singing to the Kodály hand signs will guide them towards the correct pitch. Singing into a tuner is a good way to know if you're pitching accurately.

One type of performance practised within the deaf community is signed singing, and some deaf people make an art form of this by poeticising the words in order that the signing is artistic. This can be a very enjoyable and worthwhile activity for the whole class. A teacher can contact the local centre for deaf people to ask if someone can come into school and teach the class a short signed song.

These pupils may knock instruments out of tune and be generally unaware of dynamics. Placing grains on a drum can teach awareness of dynamics.

Pupils with hearing impairments are going to want to be up there on stage performing with the rest of their classmates, but it will be harder in general for them to stay in time and pitch with the others. Obviously, pupils with severe hearing difficulties will not hear applause. (The convention for applause in the deaf community is to wave hands in the air, not to clap – this is something that schools may like to consider if they have pupils with HI.) They will rely on their signer rather than the teacher, not looking directly at the teacher or band leader.

Performances give pupils with visual impairments the chance to shine. They are not distracted by unnecessary visuals, though they may be distracted by lesser noises that other pupils will filter out (e.g. the sound of distant car horns or the central heating). However, they do live in the real world and should be able to concentrate on their own performance given adequate practice.

Visually impaired pupils will need assistance initially with finding their way around the music room and various instruments, and will need appropriate help from their support staff until they have learned where everything is and gained confidence. In the case of public performance – especially outside school – appoint a partner for the VI pupil to make sure s/he has appropriate support in unfamiliar surroundings and is kept safe. The sense of occasion will be different for pupils with visual impairment, but no less exciting; they will need to be alerted to the size of the audience and trained to face forward and how to be part of a stage team.

Performing for pupils with communication difficulties/ASD

Liberated from the need for conventional language, pupils with semantic pragmatic disorder should be more on a level with their mainstream peers during performing sessions. They may find great satisfaction in singing chunks of text.

Pupils with Asperger's syndrome sometimes have a particular focus for music and may be skilled at playing an instrument and relish performing. These pupils are sometimes able to compose intricate pieces of music, which can be almost impossible to play (especially if they are created on a computer). However, the pupil may be greatly distressed if even one note of his composition is played incorrectly.

A pianist in Town X played a piece which was written by a 15-year-old boy with autism. He had envisaged it a lot faster than she played it, not realising that it was almost impossible for anyone except a top class performer – or perhaps a computer. (Apparently Bartok was like this – every piece was timed to the second and had to be performed accurately.) The boy was distraught that his composition had been realised wrongly, and not exactly as he had written it.

In the classroom, pupils with autism may find it difficult to accept direction from an unfamiliar adult. They need to develop coping routines or explore music through intensive interaction, doing paired work with their support assistant or with another pupil from the class – see Wendy Prevezer's work about musical interaction, e.g. Prevezer (2002). A pupil with autism who is due to perform a piece at a public concert may withdraw at the eleventh hour – make sure that you always have a substitute standing by. All of these pupils may find the idea of being watched by an audience very disturbing. They should not be offered for performance unless their teachers, support staff and parents/carers feel confident that this is a good idea. Even so, there should be an escape route planned.

The school concert

Here is the dilemma. The concert is where the public sees the school, where prospective parents/carers can compare high schools, where the rest of the school views what the music department has been doing. The concert should be where the pupils present what they can do, what they have learned and what they have practised. Should you audition? If so, what would be your criteria for letting people up on stage, and should you set different rules for pupils with SEND?

The Outside Concert

Once you have decided to take pupils with additional needs to the town hall or the local residential care home, you have to consider the risks and fill in the risk assessment paperwork. There is a danger with risk assessment forms that, once you have filled in the form, you feel that you have somehow lessened the risk. Thinking seriously about the pitfalls that different venues present is helpful. The teacher may have to conclude that some risks are too high.

There are occasions where pupils and adults with special needs get together musically and exclusively. Pupils and their carers, parents and support workers appreciate these events where all the musical activities are geared towards those with SEND, and they all can compare notes. In the north of England there is YAMSEN: SpeciallyMusic (see References, resources and further information for details) and the Wharfedale Festival which has a category for entrants with SEND.

Composing

Composition benefits from pupils having improvised first, and from having listened to music from all genres and all parts of the world, and from different times (i.e. as broad a range as possible), both recorded and live. However, when composing a piece of music, what is important is very much what is in a student's head and not what they can play themselves. And of course if you are composing for a rock band, or other ensemble, inevitably you have to ask other class members to play the parts that you can't. This has several benefits for the students with additional needs:

- it helps them interact in a realistic, meaningful and not artificial way with other students;
- it allows pupils to acknowledge and celebrate what others can do;
- it allows their composition to be free of the constraints of the physically impossible.

Composing for pupils with autism or Asperger's syndrome

The way in for a lot of students on the autistic spectrum is very often on the computer, iPad or another electronic device. These often provide not just one sound at a time but one riff or chord or rhythm, which for the technologically inclined is a treasure trove.

Chris's journey started with some difficulties. Undiagnosed at that time with autism and abused at an early age, he was placed in a children's home and sent to a primary school for children with BESD. Here is part of his story (the full account is on our website):

(Continued)

Undoubtedly, my life has been transformed and saved through the sheer power of music. I am now an associate composer of the London College of Music with several grades in piano and an approaching assessment for my diploma in singing . . . I was a very angry boy, and I would be restrained or placed in a school padded cell on a daily basis . . . It became very clear early on that music provided an enormous amount of therapeutic benefit and safety to a lonely small boy . . . by the age of 16 I was a musician who was involved in music every single day. I composed pieces for orchestra, singers and various ensembles. I then went on to university . . .

Music turned an angry hurt boy with abandonment issues into a sensitive and feeling individual. I am so grateful that certain people were able to touch me with their noise so that I could become who I now am.

See www.routledge.com/9781138231849.

Composing for pupils with challenging behaviour

When working with children with EBD and on live instruments, it is advisable to have a selection of suggested structures as starting points. Some examples are provided below:

- Ask the students to devise a four bar melody (or something even shorter) using notes only from one key (and that could be pentatonic), then ask them to put chords behind, using what they can of musical theory, or just give them the two, three or four suggested chords. This would then turn into theme and variations, by turning the notes around or repeating the melody in different ways, or on different instruments.
- Give them a grid either 4 or 8 or 16 bars long and 4, 8 or 16 pieces of card with the chords from any given key on. Ask the pupils to arrange them in any order, and then experiment playing them until they find an order to suit. The preset chords on piano keyboards (triggered by playing a single note when the keyboard is set to chord mode) would be useful here, and the record facilities give students a chance to listen back and refine their work. When they are happy with their choice, they can then ask guitarists or pianists to realise the work acoustically for them.

Some pupils will never be happy and will not make a decision about a preferred chord sequence, as they find it hard to settle on any one task and stick to it. If this is a GCSE composition, it is always advisable to photocopy one of their early versions in case they rip the written version up, declaring, 'It's no good!'

Composing for pupils with MLD

For students with MLD it is best first to introduce them to a selection of tuned and untuned instruments, then create a storyboard and allow them to take a section each and create the music for each section of the story. Use graphic notation to represent their music.

Composing for pupils with physical or sensory impairments

Not all pupils with physical difficulties want to make music. However, this is sometimes because they have never been given the right equipment to make it an interesting and worthwhile activity. With the use of switches, soundbeams, iPads and suitable software, pupils can compose music on equal terms, learn to develop musical skills and create their own compositions at all levels.

Students who are visually impaired may be able to use Braille notation – but recording each part of their composition as they go along may be the best way to do this. Students with hearing impairments should be able to follow whatever the rest of the class is doing.

Composing for pupils with SLD and PMLD

For students with SLD and PMLD it is best to use switches and create sound effects or short repeated patterns associated with each one. You and the student decide on symbols to represent each different sound or riff. Then the TA places them onto a blank grid, after which they should be able to play and replay their composition until they are satisfied with the sequences of notes or riffs (see Corke, 2002).

Conclusion

Listening, improvising, performing and composing are really all that music in school is about. The rest – working with the TAs, managing the lessons, setting up the classroom, etc. – is just how a teacher manages these four components.

Some students, and some teachers, will undoubtedly prefer one part of the course to another, but which parts a student prefers will not depend on their ability or disability but on previous experience, natural inclinations and, to some extent, the teacher's ability to enthuse and to create the right environment for learning.

If handled correctly, school music lessons can set a person up for life as a professional or amateur musician; as someone who plays an instrument for themselves, as a hobby and a form of relaxation; or simply as someone who enjoys and appreciates music for its life-enhancing qualities. All of this is irrespective of any additional needs. Music lessons can help all pupils to develop the skills and qualities to enable them to live and work creatively and always be open to new ideas.

6 Lesson management

Pupils learn in different ways at different times, and unpredictably at different times of the day. How you manage your lessons, the rules, techniques and resources you use, must acknowledge this fact and combine in a way that leads to student learning and progress. This can be a tall order for music teachers who see their pupils for (at best) one hour a week, or two hours for GCSE groups. This allows limited time to get to know pupils as individuals and presents particular challenges for establishing positive relationships with learners who have special/additional needs.

This chapter, about managing the music lesson, is a realist's charter.

Methods and approaches

The music teacher has to accommodate a wide range of learning needs. One pupil will be saying 'Show me'; one pupil will be demanding the written music; another will need a different type of notation (maybe asking for the letters to be written under the notes); another may need to clap out a phrase of music before they are able to play it on their chosen instrument. Guitarists with dyslexia will probably prefer tablature over Western notation.

When you include pupils in the class with different forms of SEND, you will start to consider what is the best way to learn for each individual, and how you, the teacher, can support them in this. Table 6.1 outlines the main types of approach to learning and teaching.

Hafsah was working with a group of students exclusively with Asperger's syndrome. She handed out individual chime bars and asked them to play the notes that she named. The notes were clearly marked on the chime bars. The children could read but all to no avail. Eventually Hafsah sang the notes she needed. The students played them back.

(Continued)

Table 6.1 Approaches to teaching and learning

Type of learning/ teaching	Brief description
Aural	Students learn to play music by listening to someone else play, and copying it. Without perfect pitch or relative pitch this does not come easily. It is usually accompanied by the students watching where the teacher places her fingers etc. However, for a disproportionate number of students with SEND (especially those with Asperger's syndrome), this may be the best way, in fact the only way, to learn. (See Hafsah's story.)
Kinaesthetic	Students learn by moving their body, clapping and stamping; very useful for rhythm work, tempo and phrasing, essential for asserting silences or rests. Pitch can be demonstrated by teacher and students tapping lower and upper parts of the body to correspond with lower and higher pitched notes. Very useful also for those with dyslexia, see BDA in References, resources and further information.
Multi-sensory	Students learn through all senses, using lights, smells, touch and taste in order to enhance their musical experiences.
Notation	Traditional notation (including Braille notation) is difficult to teach properly in a class, but other types of notation are available and easier to learn. These include graphic notation (in which pictures can be used to express sounds), guitar tab (in which notes as dots are written on a visual representation of guitar strings on the frets), ocarina notation (in which an ocarina is represented as a line drawing and dots are written over the holes to be covered), Foxwood Song Sheets (in which notes and chords are written only as letters and presented in grids).
Theory	Teaching students the theory of how melodies work helps them to learn what notes or chords are likely to come next in a song. They develop understanding about different keys and modes, how rhythm can be written down, what chords and what notes to expect in a key, how to construct major and minor chords, etc.
Visual	Working visually is usually combined with working aurally, where watching someone else's hands confirms the chords or notes that the student is hearing. This is easily done if teacher and student are playing the same instrument, but it is not impossible to watch a guitarist, for example, and then play the same chords on a piano. Kodály's hand signs might also be considered to be working visually as an aid to learning.
Intellectual	For some pupils, having a diagram or even a full score showing the structure of a piece can help them learn the music and know when and how they themselves will be playing. This might include: what everyone else is playing, the shape of the melody, how the keys change, how the different melodic parts relate, what instruments play in different sections. This can apply to simple pieces where different members of the group join in at different times, or the music has repeated sections, up to understanding the voicing in a complex fugue.

I've recently seen a huge increase in the number of students using technology to support their learning but even more so to replace instrumental lessons. Students who receive no tuition manage to learn complex pieces by watching YouTube videos of someone's hands playing. No musical notation is shown, only the hands and sometimes a keyboard piano roll diagram which highlights which keys are being pressed. Popular video games like 'Guitar Hero' are influencing how people learn to play. I have tried on a few occasions now to learn a piece using this method and find it impossible!

Suzanne Peers, Head of Music and Specialist
Leader in Cultural Education
www.youtube.com/watch?v=Hk-K_D8Zz5Q
www.youtube.com/watch?v=tNM6LIH6vko

Notation

Notation was used originally as an aide-mémoire to show the direction of the melody. Gradually colours and shapes were introduced, and over the centuries the sophisticated system that is Western notation evolved. Along with notation a curious degree of musical snobbery has arisen. Notation is seen as the only way to approach Western music, while learning aurally seems acceptable for jazz, folk and world music. For any student wishing to pursue a musical career, understanding traditional Western notation is essential, as are private or peripatetic lessons. There are some gifted children, especially on the autistic spectrum, to whom staff notation comes easily, but others find it extremely challenging. Many teachers are adamant that they are teaching notation during lessons, yet a quick look around the classroom will tell you that, besides having the piece of music in front of them, the students have the letter names under the 'dots' and are demanding to hear how each section is played and asking teachers to show them what to do. (See the website resources for 'Colour coding of chords': www.routledge.com/9781138231849.)

Graphic notation is where students choose their pictures to represent sounds, either notes or clusters of notes. This is often used for improvisation and is a relaxed, imprecise science.

The Liggins' *ocarina diagrams* suit many children with additional needs. Diane Paterson's experience with deaf children was that they couldn't hear the ocarinas but loved playing them because they enjoyed using the ocarina box notation so much (www.routledge.com/9781138231849).

Twinkle, twinkle little star

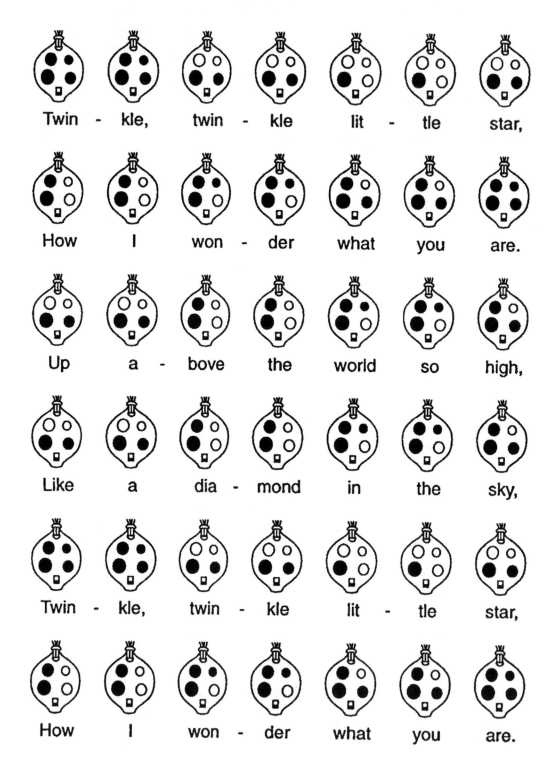

Figure 6.1 A typical piece of ocarina notation.

OcPix™ copyright 1998 D&C Liggins – www.ocarina.co.uk.

Guitar tab is a visual representation of the six strings (or however many) of a guitar, usually with bar lines, where the number of the fret to be pressed down is written on the string to be played. It is always for a right-handed player. A left-handed player must read it in reverse and can always write it the right way up for him/herself. It doesn't clearly define the duration of notes, but a guitarist would need only to hear the music once to grasp the general idea. Its logicality would appeal to those on the autistic spectrum, and its simplicity to everyone else.

Figure 6.2 Guitar tab.

Guitar boxes are a line drawing representation of the first four frets on a guitar (again, a right-handed one) with dots to show the player which frets to hold for which chord, always also naming the chord.

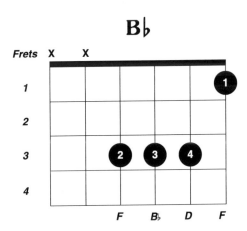

Figure 6.3 Guitar box.

The **Foxwood Song Sheets** were devised by me (VJ) whilst teaching at Foxwood School, where it was obvious that very few pupils arrived from their primary schools with any basic core musical knowledge, experience, understanding or skills. The school served a very underprivileged area and challenging behaviour was a defining feature, so delayed gratification was to be avoided wherever possible. Like guitar tab, the Song Sheets reduce the notes and chords to be played to an absolute minimum, and use a combination of grids, capital letters

1   This system of notation was devised and developed, primarily but not exclusively, for steel pans in the 1980s by Victoria Jaquiss, then Head of Music at Foxwood School.

2   Designed to support the aural tradition, it is deliberately imprecise.

3   Chords are represented by large outline capitals. Minor chords are stripey. Teacher and players can choose their rhythms.

4   The melody is in the smaller boxes. The position of a note within the bar gives an indication of its value. A little straight line, either at the top or the bottom of a melody note, emphasises either high or low pitch.

5   In order that sharps and flats take up no more space than naturals the flat or sharp symbol is attached to the note letter.

6   Wavy lines indicate held notes [pannists should roll these].

7   A box at the side tells you what notes are in which chord. Suggested bass notes are underlined.

8   Chords are colour-coded as follows:

C = red, G = green, F = yellow, D = blue, B flat = pink,
A = orange, E flat = purple, E = brown

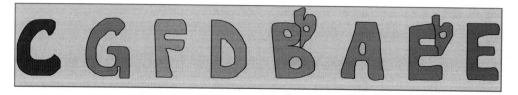

9   See the Manual for full details of how to read and write your own Foxwood Song Sheets.

10   To obtain further copies of the Manual and Song Sheet books contact Lindsay Music by email at **sales@lindsaymusic.co.uk**.

Figure 6.4 How to read the Song Sheets.

and common sense (see Figures 6.4 and 6.5 and the example sheets, in colour, on the website: www.routledge.com/9781138231849).

The Song Sheets are an aide-mémoire; they allow for improvisation and rein-terpretation and are designed to work within the aural tradition. It takes about five minutes to learn how to read and rather longer to learn to write them.

On attending a recent NASEN course about speech, language and communication needs (SLCN), I was interested to hear Wendy Lee describe how a lot of problems in inner city secondary schools, where she has done research as a speech and language therapist, have their origins in the pupils' lack of language skills. They have a limited vocabulary which can restrict understanding and effective communication. She described approaches that could be used in the classroom to simplify instructions and lead to better understanding. The Foxwood Song Sheets do exactly

(Continued)

Figure 6.5 Song Sheet example. Song Sheet design © Victoria Jaquiss 2010.

this. They were developed in such a school as Wendy describes and break down the information into its most basic need-to-know form. The information is written to show bar length, the spacing of melody notes explaining but not notating rhythm. They are set out to show the structure of the piece – there is nothing random about the layout of the page. Their most noticeable feature is the use of colours to show chords – if the instrument is prepared with matching small coloured dots on the notes, then all those who can see colours can play very quickly, and do so on a weekly basis!

Diane Paterson

Whatever notation a teacher uses, it must be remembered that notation is not an end in itself but a very useful tool that students can use when they are on their own, without the support of a teacher.

Figure 6.6 'Don't worry about the theory, Miss, just tell me what notes to play.'

Specific methods

Over the last 200 years many methods and approaches have been developed to make the learning of musical skills and creativity more accessible and to improve the quality of music making. These include Kodály, Dalcroze Eurthymics, Orff, Suzuki and Musical Futures. Some knowledge of these may enlarge the music teacher's repertoire of teaching techniques, but they would have to attend one of the many courses that run on these themes. This could be a great and enjoyable thing to do but can be costly. One of the benefits is that a teacher can then tap into a network of others out there who are already using these ideas.

These pedagogies look at child development and model their teaching of music on this. When working with children with SEND, breaking down the musical learning process in ways used by these pedagogies can be extremely effective. These children may be struggling with language, communication, physical tasks, reading, social interactions. If their music teacher can take the most appropriate ideas from these methods and approaches, they will have a bank of resources that they can use to unlock the students' musicality.

In many ways the key to success here is the enthusiasm and skill of the individual teacher and their department. Such a teacher will be familiar with different ways of teaching music and will also be perceptive about the musical abilities and need of the pupils in their class, inspiring them to learn.

Genres and appropriate selection of music

Of all school subjects, music is cursed with the idea (from other teachers, parents, governors and the general public) that the lessons will be fun. For that reason, students sometimes arrive expecting fun and are disappointed if they are asked to work at something. I usually have to tell a class some time within the first few weeks that music is a lesson and not a leisure activity.

Of course, teachers, as in all other subjects, will be searching for the best way to engage students' interest, and as music has a less precise curriculum, it is possible and tempting to turn to the students' own music preferences. This can be either as a way in or as a reward at the end of the lesson or course (usually our preference).

If pop music is used, however, there can be a problem with endlessly repeated notes in the melody, and the very few chords in the chord sequences. Take, for example, 'Da Doo Ron Ron' (well past its prime, of course): it has only three chords and only three notes in the melody. In G these chords are G, C and D, and in melody it is either G, A or B. So, selecting pieces of music to use with pupils must often rest with the teacher. I have this notice on my music room wall and read it aloud frequently:

> **You can please some of the people all of the time, and all of the people some of the time, but you can't please all of the people all of the time, so just learn this song even if you don't like it!**
>
> **Abraham Lincoln, Bob Dylan, Victoria Jaquiss**

In making these choices, teachers may get hung up about *age appropriateness*. But the high school music teacher may find her/his Y7 pupils are beginners in so many ways that 8 or 16 bar nursery rhymes are a good start. Songs like 'Twinkle, Twinkle Little Star' tend to be in most children's memory and they always find it satisfying to get right. It is entirely up to the teacher to present it carefully. These are some of the 'ways in' that have worked for us:

- This is a children's nursery rhyme. You're going to hate it. Let's just do it and get it over with.
- We are going to play a concert for Primary School X, so we need to learn some children's songs.
- I know you want to learn X's latest hit, but before we can do that, you need some skills. Although this is a children's song, it requires useful skills, for example quick chord changes and melodic leaps.
- As a composing exercise, I want you to choose a nursery rhyme, rewrite the lyrics and decide on how to orchestrate it.

Decades of experience show that pupils of all ages enjoy and get satisfaction from these classic old short tunes. (In fact, pop songs often include snippets of these melodies, e.g. the first two lines of Gotye's hit 'Somebody That I Used to Know' in the early 2010s is just 'Baa Baa Black Sheep'; the theme tune to the Flintstones movies has new lyrics to the tune of 'This Old Man'.)

Behaviour management

A lot of behaviour management in schools seems to revolve around identifying poor behaviour, naming offenders and even writing up their names on a board for all to see. It is attention for all the wrong reasons. What could be more counter-productive! With behaviour management there are three main rules:

1. Prepare in advance.
2. Ignore any behaviour that doesn't impede the flow of the lesson.
3. Keep up the pace.

Rules and routines

It is questionable whether students study the clearly displayed classroom *rules*, but they are useful for referring to and well worth discussing at some point.

Good behaviour management would involve teacher and students coming up with their own list. This is not so easy for the once-a-week music teacher, but it may be worth the initial loss of a lesson in order to agree with the students how the lessons will run. Rules are generally effective when students have ownership of them. These are equally important for all groups and can be displayed as simple picture versions (PECs) which show clearly what is expected.

Routines are essential in the inclusive music lesson. Some children have chaotic lives outside school and while they might initially fight against the routines and rules within the classroom, they usually come to accept them and value the security they give.

However, how a teacher deals with an individual's anti-social and attention-seeking behaviour depends on understanding the causes for and the most appropriate response to the behaviour. In some schools, the Behaviour Support Unit gives all heads of department a set of individual behaviour plans, which outline probable behaviour and the best solutions. Alison, for example, may be asked to 'cool off for five minutes' if her temper gets the better of her in class, after which she will return and apologise. For a similar offence, the appropriate sanction for Haleema may be a phone call to her parents at home.

In some classes there may be a high number of pupils with challenging behaviour, and the music teacher may feel that the class is unmanageable. At this point the teacher may have to consider whether all the techniques in the world are ever going to get this class to work together. And of course this situation is particularly difficult in music lessons, where there is care of equipment to consider and where listening and creation of moods are important. Proper resourcing, especially of the human variety, can help, but so can good organisation and appropriate structuring of lessons. Every lesson should be a well-organised lesson with a clear beginning (starter), middle and ending (plenary/performance), and before they leave the room, the pupils should be back sitting down at their desks with their work collected in.

The pupils should have a clear idea of what they are to study. It's a good idea to have the lesson title and aim displayed on a flip chart or whiteboard. We also recommend that pupils make a note in their music folders and their planners of the aims and outcomes (intended and otherwise).

Rules, ignore, praise

This is a very prescriptive and highly effective behaviour tool, on which most present day behaviour management is based. Essentially it is based on five elements:

1. Agreeing a set of classroom rules with the students. If the rules are adhered to, the lesson ends ten minutes early with time for negotiated activities.
2. Using what may seem like an unnaturally high rate of rule-related praise. This should also be varied and imaginative and directed at a named person or small group. Praise should be for both behaviour and academic achievement and should be consistently applied.
3. Ignoring behaviour that does not disrupt the lesson, or pose a threat to others. The danger of using 'ignoring' on its own as a tactic is that you run the risk of escalating the behaviour that is being ignored, especially if the behaviour is an attempt to seek attention. Therefore, ignoring unwanted behaviour must be used in conjunction with giving praise to someone else for appropriate named behaviour.
4. Warnings and reprimands should be used if praise–ignore fails. These should be given calmly, with the consequence coherent and clear. Body language is important; it should convey authority and not aggression. Warnings should never be repeated.
5. The ultimate consequence will be separation/time out, where the students move from a rewarding activity to an unrewarding or boring one. In a music lesson it is easy enough to remove a beater or an instrument for a minute. Time out has to be in conjunction with whole school policy. It is a negative activity which essentially allows the pupil involved to cool down, and should not be overused.

Table 6.2 and Appendix 4 provide 'at a glance' guidelines for effective behaviour management in music.

For some individuals, a personal record of behaviour targets and achievement can be useful, and we have included an example in Appendix 5.

Pace

If you want to kill a lesson off before it even starts, explain in detail at the start what you are about to do; if you want to confuse pupils with SEND, especially those on the autistic spectrum and with VI or dyspraxia, launch into the lesson without explanation. Aim for something between these two extremes; put a title and a brief explanation on the board and keep the verbal introduction to a bare minimum. You can offer ready-prepared instruction sheets to some individuals, which will get them started straight away. As the information is there for the student and TA to read, taking as long over it as they need, those who need time will have plenty.

Pace does not mean speaking quickly but involves minimal instruction and progressing to the next stage without leaving anyone behind or keeping anyone back. The Foxwood Song Sheets are useful here: they are differentiated in themselves and students can pick which parts they need on the day.

It is generally acknowledged that most pupils can concentrate for about 20 minutes, so it is advisable to change activity within a music lesson every 15 to 20 minutes, unless that magic moment arrives when the whole class is absorbed in what it is doing. By sustaining good pace in lessons, you will avoid boredom and frustration and maintain pupils' interest and motivation. Always plan 'more than enough' so that if pupils surprise you in completing quickly, you have something else prepared.

The tips in Table 6.2 offer handy reminders for music teachers in schools and music centres.

Table 6.2 Good behaviour management in music

Do	*Don't*
Learn pupils' names	Muddle through with 'you boy' etc.
Tell them what the lesson's aim is, maybe also put the aim on display	Launch into the lesson with no explanation
Look to praise good behaviour – catch them being good	Describe aloud behaviour that you don't want to see
Explain the rules, and praise **honestly** (ideally at a rate of 30 praise statements to 5 criticisms per session)	Say 'well done' when it wasn't
Record work on tape, on paper, by video and photographs	Limit ways of recording success
Provide certificates – sometimes publicly awarded for work well done, help offered to peers, etc.	Devalue rewards by overusing them
Leave tasks and materials for them to practise during the week	Abandon something that the pupils may have been looking forward to
Give students responsibilities to suit their needs and abilities	Force people into roles they can't handle
Speak to everybody separately at least once	Give all your attention to attention-seeking, badly behaved pupils
Give them bits of theory as soon as they are ready	Overdo the theory at the expense of enjoyment and satisfaction
Have something ready to include late-comers without needing to speak to them	Pay any overt attention to late-comers
Entertain and impress them with your own instrument playing	Bore them or make them feel inadequate with your own playing
Tell support staff what you want them to do	Expect support staff to read your mind

(Continued)

Table 6.2 continued

Do	Don't
Keep the pace snappy and change task every 10–20 minutes	Spend too long on any one task
Reinforce and repeat	Move on too quickly
Pick up swiftly on bullying, racism, etc., express disapproval, get on with music	Overreact to minor misdemeanours
Change direction of lesson if it seems appropriate	Get sidetracked by answering unrelated questions, however musical or fascinating, which will hold up your lesson
Ensure that each lesson includes a satisfying musical experience	Lose track of time
Have a series of sanctions that allow the pupils to 'start again' (e.g. a minute sitting out)	Make threats you can't or won't carry out
Own up if you make a mistake	Attempt to give the impression that you are infallible
Question everything	Assume anything
Get to know what sort of music pupils like, and respect their taste	Try to impose your own tastes on them
Be careful about how you refer to pupils' home lives	Assume they have two parents at home, have a computer, have a car
Remember you are there to empower them on their route to independence	Encourage pupils to be unnecessarily dependent

Sending students with SEND for peripatetic music lessons

Students with special/additional needs and disabilities have as much right to 'peri' lessons as anyone else. Who gets the lessons may depend on school policy, student or parental choice, whether they are in the GCSE Music class, or even the music teacher's whim or educated guess.

Peripatetic music teachers should be given information about any pupils with SEND and appropriate support in meeting their needs, possibly with additional adult support. Some pupils, for example those on the autistic spectrum or with challenging behaviour, should not usually be alone with a visiting teacher. You may want to check on the peripatetic teacher's experience and qualifications in this respect, and take advice from the SENCO. Consider the mix of pupils in any tuition group and monitor their progress: one pupil may streak ahead, another lag behind and possibly hold others back. Make an effort to visit a lesson – ask another teacher to supervise your regular class for ten minutes if needed.

Conclusion

Whatever methods, styles and techniques a teacher employs in the music lesson, their aim should be to:

1. teach the students to **play and appreciate** music to the best of their abilities, building on previous lessons and anticipating what activities can happen in the future;
2. *inspire* those with an obvious need and/or talent to take music further;
3. provide the stimuli for students to *enjoy and appreciate* a wide range of music.

7 Working with teaching assistants

At the time of writing, support staff numbers stand at around a quarter of a million (full-time equivalent) in the 23,000 schools in England (National Statistics, April 2014). Support staff may be called by different names in different authorities: teaching assistants (TAs), special support assistants, pupil assistants, statement support assistants or learning support assistants (LSAs). Their role is to help teachers and to work with other professionals such as speech and language therapists and parents to support children's learning. Some are allocated to an individual pupil with special needs as part of their education, health and care plan (EHCP), while others support a whole class or groups within the class. Support staff may also provide administrative support or technical support, or be involved in pastoral care. More often than not these days, they have received formal training.

Essentially their presence in the classroom should enable you to teach the whole class and its individuals better than if they were not there, and they should enable the student with an EHCP to get the most out of the lesson.

The relationship between teacher and TA is important to get right, but not always easy. If you both work at the school all the time, you will see each other out of the lesson and be able to discuss students' individual needs before and after the music lessons. If you are a visiting peripatetic music teacher who meets the class and teaching assistant once a week, it can be problematic. The teacher will know the subject matter, the assistant will know the student, but there will be no time to discuss any matters arising, as, when the bell sounds, one will be with the next class, and the other will be at the next school.

There will be times when a student with additional needs is in your lesson and does have a teaching assistant 'permanently attached'. The teacher needs to be aware of these situations and plan how to manage the time in music lessons – for both the student and the TA. There is a useful check list in Table 7.1 for the music teacher to offer the TA so that the latter has some idea of what is expected of them.

Table 7.1 Inclusive checklist for TAs in music

MUSIC: Performing, composing, listening with **pupils who have physical difficulties**

Instruments and equipment	Teaching method/support
Do • Find something to fit on the wheelchair tray, e.g. single octave keyboard or mini-keys keyboard • Use height adjustable tables • Use keyboard midi linked to PC with appropriate music software and switches **Don't** • Worry if a pupil spends the whole lesson on one instrument and/or plays in an unusual way	**Do** • Leave the pupil in full control of the activity whenever possible • Try to ascertain their tastes • Establish effective communication – possibly eye pointing for choosing **Don't** • Do the work for them • Look over the pupil's shoulder throughout the activity • Impose your own musical tastes
Activities	**Plenary**
Do • Set tasks as for the rest of the class, but allow more time to experiment • Expect aversion to some sounds • Be patient and persevere **Don't** • Rush them • Force them to 'perform' if they are unwilling	**Do** • Record onto sequencer (maybe in step time), write or type onto computer • Encourage to participate in any way they are comfortable with **Don't** • Pass them by

MUSIC: Performing, composing, listening with **pupils who have behaviour difficulties**

Instruments and equipment	Teaching methods
Do • Let pupil have free choice of instrument, but take care with delicate equipment • Make sure loud instruments are not played at top volume • Ensure they know where all their music, plectrums, sticks and beaters are kept • Have a ready supply of pens and pencils for those who come without **Don't** • Allow them to bully others off an instrument • Let them dominate/disrupt the lesson	**Do** • Give firm, clear instructions • Stay with the pupil until they have understood the task • Frequently remind them of school and music room rules • Demonstrate good listening skills yourself • Put your fingers to your mouth to indicate silence **Don't** • Give them too much choice or an overflexible brief • Talk at all while music is being played, even to reply to the pupil

(Continued)

Activities	Plenary
Do	**Do**
• Use easy keys to start with (A on guitar, C on keyboards, etc.) • Be very patient when introducing new ideas • Manage seating arrangements appropriately (split up troublemakers, provide good role models)	• Give plenty of warning that the end of the lesson is coming and stay with them while they write up and/or record their performance
Don't	**Don't**
• Let pupils change instruments too often, i.e. just after they have started getting somewhere • Let them wander off task	• Take over responsibility for writing up the notes for pupils

MUSIC: Performing, composing and listening with **pupils who have hearing impairments**

Instruments and equipment	Teaching methods
Do	**Do**
• Work with wooden sounds and drums as first choice • Have good amplification for electronic instruments • Make sure they can see any instruments being demonstrated	• Use visual clues during listening activities • Check hearing aids • Make sure the pupil can see your/ the teacher's face when instructions/ explanations are being given • Have an alternative activity if they cannot hear the CD • Use signs and graphic scores and notation • Work in pairs/small groups
Don't	**Don't**
• Use too many instruments which resonate for a long time, e.g. gongs • Allow them to knock the instruments out of tune	• Have low expectations
Activities	**Plenary**
Do	**Do**
• Find out what they can and cannot hear • Have lots of rhythm work • Learn to sign the songs • Use a soundproof area for practical work if possible	• Expect enthusiastic performances • Limit the amount of extraneous noise
Don't	**Don't**
• Assume that pupils with HI can't do music • Avoid melody work	• Discourage them from taking part

MUSIC: Performing, composing, listening with **pupils who have visual impairments**

Instruments and equipment	Teaching methods
Do • Allow free choice of instruments • Use personal tape recorder or mini-disk player • Allow pupil to use personal laptop (with screen-reader) • Make them aware of what instruments are available in the room • Mark instruments with tactile markers **Don't** • Hand over the pupil's instruments without warning • Play sudden loud sounds • Use poor quality or out of tune instruments	**Do** • Leave the pupil in full control of the activity where possible • Be on hand to help find equipment • Be ready to help record instructions and musical examples onto tape **Don't** • Assume that they will need help in recording • Assume they will have a perfect musical memory
Activities **Do** • Set tasks as for the rest of the class • Find a soundproof area to work in during practical sessions **Don't** • Talk while they are working	**Plenary** **Do** • Have high expectations **Don't** • Bypass these pupils

MUSIC: Performing, composing, listening with **pupils who have autistic spectrum disorders**

Instruments and equipment	Teaching methods
Do • Encourage to try out a new instrument **Don't** • Worry if they always use the same instrument • Worry if they play in an unusual way	**Do** • Keep on task • Allow to go into depth with one task **Don't** • Overload them • Let them ruin the lesson for other pupils
Activities **Do** • Listening activities as for the rest of the class • Find a soundproof area to work in during practical sessions when possible • Expect aversion to some sounds • Be patient and persevere **Don't** • Force the pupil to be part of an ensemble if it's proving difficult • Give up on them	**Plenary** **Do** • Record onto tape or into computer for playback • Expect in-depth answers – or no answer at all **Don't** • Push them to perform in front of an audience

Whatever the TA's educational training and experience, the arts, especially music lessons, present certain challenges. Many support staff will come from the time when music was regarded as a talent, not a school subject available to all, and will often preface their presence in your classroom with the opinion that they are 'not musical'. Do they venture into humanities, I wonder, with the words, 'I am not geographical'?

However confident they feel, TAs will need guidance from the teacher about their role in the music lesson and the ways in which they can support pupils. Julie, an ex-student who is presently training to be a TA, wrote these notes about her course:

The main things were that we had to have two observations on us while carrying out a task set by the teacher (guided reading, a maths task, etc.) with a small group of children. Then we had to do an observation on a child in the class to track their development. We had a basic background on milestones at certain ages, and development learned through the acronym PILES (physical, intellectual, language, emotional, social). We had to make sure we understood and could summarise school policies, had knowledge of how to safeguard, where the first aid kits were, etc. We had units on a safe environment in school, how to effectively communicate with children and adults, identifying childhood illnesses, how to support learning, supporting children with maths, and rules and dealing with challenging behaviour.

When I asked Julie about specific subject instructions, she wrote this:

Yes. I was told to just sit with them and try to keep them engaged in the lesson and work they were given and what their specific goals were to achieve that lesson.

TAs should be aware that Music doesn't have 'specific goals' as such. Music lessons should be voyages of discovery, with a general aim, e.g. 'Find a song you would like to learn and see how far you get with it.' If the students go off-piste, they should be allowed to follow their instincts.

One area where music differs from other subjects is in the need, at times, for total *silence*. This can be when pupils are asked to respond emotionally to a piece of music, recorded or live. There is a danger that TAs may regard their charges and themselves as exempt from this silence. The TA may even feel that she is 'not earning her money' if she merely sits and listens to music. It is important for the teacher to discuss these issues with TAs and to establish, from the outset, a mutually beneficial way of working.

The list below provides some suggested ways in which teachers can support their TAs and maximise their input:

- Be clear about your expectations. Remember it is the teacher who is in charge of, and responsible for, the pupil and the lesson.
- Think about the TA's role when planning lessons.
- Inform the TA in advance about what the aims of the lesson will be and the tasks involved.
- Acknowledge the TA when talking to pupils – the higher their status, the more effective they can be.

Matching the support with the students

With **pupils on the autistic spectrum** assistants have possibly the hardest job of all of them, and possibly the most fun. To be effective in the music lesson they will need a working knowledge of musical interaction (see the work of Wendy Prevezer, e.g. Prevezer 2002). As it is likely that they will spend much of the day with the pupil, they will be familiar with his/her obsessions and will probably already have their own methods for encouraging task completion.

With pupils who demonstrate challenging behaviour, having someone next to them who they can distract needs thoughtful handling. The TA's role might be as much to remove them from the room when they 'kick off' as to keep them on task, but it would be better if s/he is apparently helping the class generally while paying attention to how the student is coping. Too often it may seem easier to indulge them.

The TA needs a pocket full of stationery, a dictionary full of avoidance tactics and infinite patience. They must take care not to overrule or undermine the teacher in matters of discipline and be ready to remove the pupil from the room with minimal disruption to the lesson.

Supporting pupils with learning difficulties requires a teaching assistant to step back sometimes and encourage as much independence as possible. Playing or singing alongside the pupil and demonstrating enthusiasm for the lesson provides a good role model.

Pupils with physical difficulties

Every Friday morning for half a term the support assistant would wheel William into his music lesson. Both William and the assistant loved this lesson and the teacher loved having them there. William was especially fond of improvising. He and his support assistant did this with the Alesis'sAirFX, a DJ-ing gadget which you operate partly through a soundbeam. One day just after half term William's support assistant was suddenly called out of the lesson and asked the music teacher to work with William on his own. This was when the music teacher came to realise that the support assistant had really enjoyed using the AirFX and William was desperate to have a go on the violin.

Pupils with physical difficulties can be divided into two main categories in terms of how much support they need from their teaching assistants. There are those with very limited movement who rely upon switches and iPads to connect with the outside world. Their support staff will be with them throughout their school day and deal with all their intimate requirements. Their assistant will literally be 'their right hand person' and will connect them with other people.

The good thing about these support assistants is that they are very close to the pupil and will not be afraid to tell them off, but they may also be overprotective. The music teacher should introduce new ideas gently, including the support assistant as they go and, hopefully, winning them over. If any writing is required from these pupils, the support assistant will act as amanuensis and will be expert at understanding the pupil's means of communicating.

Some of these pupils will have communication devices attached to their wheelchairs. These are effectively the child's voice and so the pupil must always control their use – just as a teacher would not cover a student's mouth to stop them speaking, so a communication device must not be switched off by a teacher or TA. If the use of communication aids is a concern, the teacher can ask for advice from the speech and language therapist.

The best assistants allow pupils to take the lead whenever possible. They will, for example, hold up two alternatives and ask the pupil to eye-point their choice. The support assistant, through their line manager, will be in constant communication with the parents and will be able to report back any successes identified by the teacher.

Secondly, there are the **pupils with such conditions as muscular dystrophy** (probably with electric wheelchairs), able to use their arms but in a limited way.

They need support staff to set up and position equipment but not to operate the equipment on the pupils' behalf.

Thirdly, there are those who have full control of the top half of their body. They will get themselves where they need to be with little help, as long as the room is set up correctly. These are the wheelchair users who will require no extra support for your lesson. This will be obvious when you meet them.

Pupils with sensory impairment

If your **pupil who is deaf or hearing impaired** comes with a signer, the pupil will watch the signer not you. Your relationship with the signer is important. If you want the pupil to take part in a singing lesson, you should give the signer the song's text well in advance so that s/he can rehearse it before the lesson. The signer may be willing to coach the pupil for a signed performance.

For **pupils who are blind or visually impaired** the TA needs only to set up the environment so that the pupil can find things easily. They might act as an amanuensis. They could make sure that the music room is labelled, where appropriate, with accessible Braille or Moon signs.

Conclusion

As inclusion becomes a reality in our schools, some support staff may be 'permanently attached' to their charges. The classroom teacher needs to be aware of these situations and plan how to manage the time in music lessons – for both the student and the TA.

It may be the case that the TA finds her/himself 'taking over' from the pupil – answering questions for him/her, setting up instruments, even playing them, rather than always encouraging the student to be as independent as possible. Alternatively, the TA may feel that she knows nothing about music and can therefore 'take a back seat in these lessons' – that she has nothing to offer. If this does happen, it really is best to tackle issues before they become entrenched behaviour. The assistant will be looking to the teacher to take the lead, and that is what the teacher must do, and with confidence.

> A peripatetic teacher was introducing djembes to a class in a particularly difficult but musical inner city school. Two women were sitting chatting at the back of the hall while the teacher set up all the instruments, chose which pupils would partner each other, and started teaching. The class teacher (who had the other half of the class next door) called in to see how things were going. The peripatetic teacher asked who the women were, because their chat was a bit distracting. 'Oh, they're support assistants,' she said, somewhat wearily.

In many instances, we have come a long way since TAs chatted at the backs of rooms, keeping an eye on their charges from a distance and offering occasional threats. But, as with all aspects of teaching, the effective deployment of support staff is something that has to be considered and planned for, and a good working relationship established.

8   Monitoring and assessment

Monitoring and assessing pupils can be motivating for the pupils themselves, to help them see what they have achieved and what else they could do. At long last, the powers that be have realised that allocating numbers isn't going to steer pupils towards their musical future. It is far better to identify what skills and what knowledge each pupil has developed and get the pupil to note these on their own record sheets (see the website for examples: www.routledge.com/9781138231849).

If teachers use record sheets like these, pupils will build up a tangible list of subjects and skills covered, and in a non-competitive and unthreatening way. This means that all pupils with SEND can easily be included and keeping notes about the names of songs learned etc. is a more dynamic and exciting way of recording achievement than having a bank of sentences beginning 'I can . . .'.

If a music teacher doesn't trust her/himself to be sure if a performance is good or not, they can consult a local 'music for additional needs' charity or Music Service for advice. However, if a student picks their way painfully through the first line of 'Ode to Joy', don't say that is fantastic when the child knows it isn't. Say, 'Well done, you have all the notes in the right order, now try to get the rhythm more even.'

Formative assessments

Most music teachers routinely record performances for individual pupils and classes on the many and various types of technology we now have available. In this way they can demonstrate progress by reminding pupils what they sounded like last year compared to what they can do now.

Students should have documentation which will identify their learning needs that are additional to and different from those accommodated in a differentiated lesson. When it comes to playing and using musical instruments and equipment, the music teacher may need to add some targets of her/his own.

It may be that a pupil will also come with a musical gift, and this should also be recognised and the student's specific needs met.

P Scales are a complex and detailed system of noting what **students with significant SEND** can do. They are common to all school subjects and, in music, will identify the slightest reaction to a musical sound, or to the point and beyond where the student becomes proactive in their interaction with musical activities (see examples below).

Performance – P Scale – attainment targets for pupils with special educational needs

July 2014

Music

Performance descriptors:

P1   (i) Pupils encounter activities and experiences. They may be passive or resistant. They may show simple reflex responses [for example, startling at sudden noises or movements]. Any participation is fully prompted.

P1   (ii) Pupils show emerging awareness of activities and experiences. They may have periods when they appear alert and ready to focus their attention on certain people, events, objects or parts of objects [for example, becoming still in a concert hall]. They may give intermittent reactions [for example, sometimes becoming excited at repeated patterns of sounds].

P2   (i) Pupils begin to respond consistently to familiar people, events and objects. They react to new activities and experiences [for example, turning towards unfamiliar sounds]. They begin to show interest in people, events and objects [for example, looking for the source of music]. They accept and engage in coactive exploration [for example, being encouraged to stroke the strings of a guitar].

P2   (ii) Pupils begin to be proactive in their interactions. They communicate consistent preferences and affective responses [for example, relaxing during certain pieces of music but not others]. They recognise familiar people, events and objects [for example, a favourite song]. They perform actions, often by trial and improvement, and they remember learned responses over short periods of time [for example,

repeatedly pressing the keys of an electronic key board instrument].
They cooperate with shared exploration and supported participation
[for example, holding an ocean drum]. . . .

P7 Pupils listen to music and can describe music in simple terms [for
example, describing musical experiences using phrases or statements combining a small number of words, signs, symbols or
gestures]. They respond to prompts to play faster, slower, louder,
softer. They follow simple graphic scores with symbols or pictures
and play simple patterns or sequences of music. Pupils listen and
contribute to sound stories, are involved in simple improvisation and
make basic choices about the sound and instruments used. They
make simple compositions [for example, by choosing symbols or picture cue cards, ordering them from left to right, or making patterns of
sounds using computer software].

P8 Pupils listen carefully to music. They understand and respond to
words, symbols and signs that relate to tempo, dynamics and pitch
[for example, faster, slower, louder, higher, lower]. They create their
own simple compositions, carefully selecting sounds. They create
simple graphic scores using pictures or symbols. They use a growing musical vocabulary of words, signs or symbols to describe what
they play and hear [for example, fast, slow, high, low]. They make and
communicate choices when performing, playing, composing, listening and appraising [for example, prompting members of the group to
play alone, in partnerships, in groups or all together].

https://www.gov.uk/government/uploads/system/uploads/
attachment_data/file/329911/Performance_-_P_Scale_-_attainment_
targets_for_pupils_with_special_educational_needs.pdf

For these pupils the *Sounds of Intent* (SOI) framework is also a vehicle for
making an assessment of musical engagement. Teachers or their assistants
log an initial assessment online and this can be followed up at regular intervals
to show progress. The SOI website has the facility to generate graphs show-
ing progress and has many online video examples of good practice. For more
information see http://soundsofintent.org/soi.html. This framework is about
more than assessment; the videos can be used to reinforce staff training and
understanding of how children's musicality can be developed.

BSquared is an assessment system which gives a list of things pupils can aim
to achieve in lessons or could be working towards, with assessment tick lists
linked to the P levels.

The only problem with tick lists and targets is that there will be spaces left unticked and targets unreached. Until we get to know our students and provide opportunities for them in a non-judgemental climate, none of us know what they will really be able to do.

I often get asked to say how to work with a pupil I've never met and my comment is I won't know until I meet them and can assess what they can do. It's common sense, but people think describing their disability will tell me a lot about how able they are at music or not. This early assessment of potential will prevent a teacher leaving a pupil with activities well below their ability.

Specialist teacher for students with additional needs

Two pupils who I know well from the school's inclusion unit were now in my mainstream music lesson. Here they have objects with them that they can play with if not coping with the lesson. I already knew that they could do all the activities I had planned – but as they were accompanied by an inexperienced TA (her first day), they misbehaved and ran to grab their safe objects – two dolls – and started messing with them. I asked them if I could have the dolls and put them out of sight. I was then able to get them to play the music like everyone else in the lesson. They joined in really well. This only worked because I already knew them, having worked with their group separately each week for several years. In this small group I've assessed their musical ability and concentration levels and come to understand their behaviour and avoidance tactics. In all this time I'd never seen the dolls.

Diane

Completing an *Arts Award* is a good way of demonstrating what pupils can achieve. It gives space for pupils to describe and reflect on arts activities they have been involved in and then set these activities in the larger picture, asking them to look at other artists and communicate what they have done with others.

It is a sort of Duke of Edinburgh Award for the arts and can be tailor-made to suit any student's abilities. It starts at Discovery level and works up through Arts Award Explore and Bronze. These are often the highest levels that pupils with learning difficulties achieve – however, some pupils may be able to do the higher awards of Silver and Gold. The Gold Arts Award carries UCAS points. There is a lot of support for these awards via the Arts Award website.

GCSE and other summative assessments

It is worth remembering that GCSEs go all the way from G up to A* (at the time of writing). There is plenty of scope and plenty of space for all students with SEND to take this particular examination. Listening, composing and performing take roughly equal marks, so anyone can still get a grade if one of them isn't a strength.

For students with challenging behaviour the A*s are the limit. With guidance on composing, students can spend as many hours a week as they need on computers, locked in a space where they don't have to interact and maybe fall out with the rest of the class. Of course we are not recommending GCSE Music for all challenging children, just for those who have demonstrated musicality in KS3.

If composition is on acoustic instruments, either let staff realise the other parts or let the student multi-track. Similarly, staff can play for these students' ensemble performances. The benefits to the students in terms of academic results that they deserve will be life long, so now is the time to give those children all the attention they crave and need.

Very occasionally, a teacher may come across a **child with ASD** who has a particular gift for music – to the point of being a 'genius' in that one area of ability. Teachers need to nurture such gifts and allow them to flourish. (See Chris Bevan's story on the website: www.routledge.com/9781138231849.)

Pupils with dyslexia, dyscalculia or dyspraxia may just need extra time. There is very little writing involved in GCSE Music; many of the questions are multiple choice so the marks lost through spelling mistakes are minimal. We strongly recommend that the music teacher does not correct spellings or even attempt to teach them. A dyslexic child never learns how to spell; they learn how to cope without spelling correctly. In order to perform, compose or appreciate music, there is no need to be able to spell. The music teacher should take the pressure off. Dyslexics include famous successful entrepreneurs and artists, and the dyslexic GCSE-taker may well achieve an A*.

For **students with physical difficulties** the real issue here is that what the pupil can hear inside their head is not what they are able to reproduce with their body, and they may have problems with performance. In order to assess and compare these pupils fairly, the teacher and the TA should allow longer for the tests, put in the notes etc. to be played in real time, and then use the program to realise their intentions. (Most sequencing programs have a step-time input.) Discuss the situation with the moderators from the exam board. But for GCSE, with allowances for amanuenses or extra time, whatever is needed, they should be more successful with other components of the exam.

For **students with sensory impairments** there are two national organisations that can help. They are Music and the Deaf and RNIB. By the time they get to GCSE Music, anyone who is profoundly deaf will be committed enough to take on the challenge. If a deaf pupil wants to go along the exam route, then the teacher should contact Music and the Deaf.

Although **blind and visually impaired pupils** will exhibit the usual full range of musical abilities, teachers may expect them to be disproportionately success-ful in music. Sight-reading forms a very small part of music exams and can be replaced by aural tests. It is possible for pupils familiar with Braille music to be tested on it.

GCSE, A level and BTec music and music technology courses have all been successfully taken by blind and partially sighted students, including those working purely aurally. This is done using the special arrangements outlined by the JCQ (Joint Council for Qualifications, from RNIB music guide, 2013). Where pupils with additional needs have reached GCSE standard and wish to enter for the exam, arrangements can be made in negotiation with the Joint Curriculum Council.

Please see the document *Access Arrangements, Reasonable Adjustments and Special Consideration* (www.jcq.org.uk/exams-office/access-arrangements-and-special-consideration/regulations-and-guidance/access-arrangements-and-reasonable-adjustments-2016-2017). For example, provision is made for extra time, scribes, signers, Braille copies, as well as cases being considered on an individual basis. The document has a comprehensive list of what is available.

Conclusion

For most students with SEND, being measured against their peers is mostly only ever going to amount to failing. Teachers should investigate and devise parallel methods of assessment and recording in order to avoid demotivating pupils in their classes who get high marks for effort on reports, but low marks for achievement.

As these students progress through school, an aptitude for music may not be reflected in other subjects, so effective tracking may throw up some interest-ing anomalies which would suggest that the very musical pupil with additional needs should be directed towards more musical activities (college courses, extra lessons, local youth groups, even more lessons in school time).

Teachers are already well aware of the dangers of grading, and the artificial and superficial conclusions that may be drawn from it. When schools have awards evenings, they generally present in-house certificates for performing at the civic hall or the local primary school, or contributing to the life of the school. They may also have certificates from their local Music Service for musical development days and concert tours.

Monitoring and assessment should be there to serve the student. Individual care plans, which are drawn up to tell staff what a pupil's difficulties and needs are, should also include a statement identifying their musical strengths (and how they will contribute to the pupil's social and learning development).

9 Some last words

It is widely believed that learning music helps young people to 'learn' in general, and that it is a 'unique form of communication', yet its place in our school curriculum hardly ever seems secure. Teachers of music have to fight constantly for a slot in the timetable. This is unfortunate because, for pupils with SEND, music can be especially valuable, not least because it provides opportunities for success when other subjects seem to offer only difficulties.

Two young people with severe physical disabilities were making music at an after-school club. One was using a head switch with a gong, the other a tilt switch with a bass drum. They were asked to play their sound and then indicate when the other person could take their turn. Unfortunately, not much sharing went on. Each pupil who took the lead forgot to ask the other to join in. Having lived their lives in isolation, and with others making every move for them, the boys had no sense of working together with others as an ensemble, nor of turn-taking. Music was about to change all that!

Music is an important part of the curriculum for pupils with SEND for a host of reasons:

- Learning music develops cognitive skills.
- Performance develops sequencing, and basic literacy and numeracy skills.
- All music involves counting.
- Playing instruments such as a gong or soundbeam develops spatial awareness.
- Singing reinforces language skills (including spelling) and lyrics can help to develop insight into different cultures, spirituality, etc. and improve self-awareness.
- Playing in an ensemble requires social awareness and an ability to co-operate.

- Music can determine mood and can aid the control and concentration of pupils.
- The pupils' own musical tastes can be acknowledged and shared, providing a way for teachers and TAs to develop a relationship with them.
- Music can be a place where pupils with SEND are on equal terms with other students.
- Pupils can achieve success and this leads to greater self-esteem.

Including pupils with SEND in your music lessons may be a challenge but it will also be very rewarding. You might need to consider some physical reorganisation of the music suite and acquire some new equipment; you will certainly need to give careful thought to how the music curriculum can be made accessible to all. This will require additional time and effort on your part but ultimately will make you a better teacher – not only a better teacher of pupils with special needs, but a better teacher of all.

Appendix 1

SEND legislation and guidance

The Children and Families Act: a different landscape

The Children and Families Act 2014 introduced radical changes to the requirements placed on both schools and teachers regarding the education and inclusion of pupils with special educational needs and disabilities. The first major revision of the SEN framework for 30 years, it introduced a new system to help children with special educational needs and disabilities and shaped how education, health and social care professionals should work in partnership with children, young people and their families.

The reforms introduced a system to support children and young people from birth up to the age of 25, designed to ensure smooth transitions across all services as they move from school into further education, training and employment. The reforms give particular emphasis to preparing children and young people for adulthood from the earliest years. This means enabling children to be involved at as young an age as possible in all decisions relating to their learning, therapy, medical treatment and support from social care. The result of this preparation should be that when young people reach the age of 16, they are able to be full and active participants in all important decisions about their life.

> There is now an important distinction made between a child and a young person. The Act gives significant new rights directly to young people when they are over compulsory school age but under the age of 25. Under the Act, a child becomes a young person after the last day of summer term during the academic year in which he or she turns 16. This is subject to a young person 'having capacity' to take a decision under the Mental Capacity Act 2005.

Throughout this book the term 'pupils with special educational needs and disabilities (SEND)' is used. A pupil has special educational needs if he or she:

- has a significantly greater difficulty in learning than the majority of others of the same age; or
- has a disability which prevents or hinders him or her from making use of facilities of a kind generally provided for others of the same age in mainstream schools or mainstream post-16 institutions.

(SEND Code of Practice 2015)

Section 19 principles

Central to Part 3 of the Children and Families Act 2014 is Section 19. This section emphasises the role to be played by parents/carers and young people themselves in all decision making about their SEND provision.

Part C of Section 19 issues a new challenge to schools in that there is a clear expectation not only that parents and pupils will be invited to participate but also that they should be supported to do so. This will certainly involve the provision of relevant information to parents, but schools could also consider providing other forms of support: both practical support, such as helping with translation services or even transport to attend important meetings, and emotional support, such as advocacy or pre-meetings to prepare parents and pupils to take a full part in all decisions. Many parents will need only a minimal level of additional support, but others – especially those often portrayed as 'hard to reach' – may require considerably more.

Key questions:

- Do you know the wishes and feelings about education of your pupils with SEND and their parents? If not, how can you find out?
- What could you and others in your subject/departmental team do to integrate this information into your planning for and delivery of teaching and learning?
- What more could you do to reach out to parents who may be anxious about or unwilling to engage with school?

The SEND Code of Practice

As the quotation at the start of this chapter makes clear, SEN provision is provision that is additional to or different from the high quality, differentiated teaching to which all pupils are entitled. A school's first response to a pupil falling behind his or her peers should be to evaluate the quality of teaching and learning the pupil currently receives in all subjects. The pupil should be identified as having SEN only when the school is confident that all teaching is differentiated appropriately to meet that individual pupil's needs.

Once a pupil is identified as having SEN, schools are required to do whatever they can to remove any barriers to learning and to put in place effective provision, or 'SEN Support'. This support must enable pupils with SEN to achieve the best possible outcomes.

Most schools and academies welcome pupils with a range of vulnerabilities, including special educational needs and disabilities, but may hesitate about including those with significant or complex needs. The reasons behind this reluctance are often a lack of expertise in an area of need, worries about behaviour and, most commonly expressed, concerns about the impact of that pupil's needs on the education of others.

The SEND Code of Practice is very clear that where the parent of a pupil with an education, health and care plan (EHC plan) makes a request for a particular school, the local authority *must* comply with that preference and name the school in the plan unless:

- it would be unsuitable for the age, ability, aptitude or SEN of the child or young person, or
- the attendance of the child or young person there would be incompatible with the efficient education of others, or the efficient use of resources.

(SEND Code of Practice 2015, 9.79, p. 172)

Legally, schools cannot refuse to admit a pupil who does not have an EHC plan because they do not feel able to cater for his or her needs, or because the pupil does not have an EHC plan.

Outcomes

Outcomes are written from the perspective of the pupil and should identify what the provision is intended to achieve. For example, do you think the following is an outcome for a pupil in Year 7 with literacy difficulties?

> For the next 10 weeks Jake will work on an on-line literacy program for 20 minutes three times each week.

It may be specific and measurable; it is achievable and realistic; and it is time targeted, so it is 'SMART' but it isn't an 'outcome'. What is described here is provision, i.e. the intervention that the school will use to help Jake to make accelerated progress.

Outcomes are intended to look forward to the end of the next stage or phase of education, usually two or three years hence. Teachers will, of course, set short term targets covering between 6 and 12 weeks, and Education and Health Plans will also include interim objectives to be discussed at annual reviews. So, what would be an outcome for Jake?

> By the end of Year 9, Jake will be able to read and understand the textbooks for his chosen GCSE courses.

The online literacy course would then form a part of the package of provision to enable Jake to achieve this outcome.

The graduated approach

The 2014 SEND Code of Practice describes SEN Support as a cyclical process of assess, plan, do and review that is known as the 'graduated approach'. This cycle is already commonly used in schools, and for pupils with SEN it is intended to be much more than a token, in-house process. Rather it should be a powerful mechanism for reflection and evaluation of the impact of SEN provision. Through the four-part cycle, decisions and actions are revisited, refined and revised. This then leads to a deeper understanding of an individual pupil's needs whilst also offering an insight into the effectiveness of the school's overall provision for pupils with SEN. The graduated approach offers the school, the pupil and his or her parents a growing understanding of needs and of what provision the pupil requires to enable him or her to make good progress and secure good outcomes. Through successive cycles, the graduated approach draws on increasingly specialist expertise, assessments and approaches, and more frequent reviews. This structured process gives teachers the information they need to match specific, evidence based interventions to pupils' individual needs.

Evidence based interventions

In recent years, a number of universities and other research organisations have produced evidence about the efficacy of a range of different interventions for vulnerable pupils and pupils with SEN. Most notable among this research is that sponsored by the Education Endowment Fund that offers schools valid data on the impact of interventions and the optimal conditions for their use. Other important sources of information about evidence based interventions for specific areas of need are the Communication Trust 'What Works?' website and 'Interventions for Literacy' from the SpLD/Dyslexia Trust. Both sites offer transparent and clear information for professionals and parents to support joint decisions about provision.

The Equality Act 2010

Sitting alongside the Children and Families Act 2014, the requirements of the Equality Act 2010 remain firmly in place. This is especially important because many children and young people who have SEN may also have a disability under the Equality Act. The definition of disability in the Equality Act is that the child or young person has 'a physical or mental impairment which has a long-term and substantial adverse effect on a person's ability to carry out normal day-to-day activities'.

'Long-term' is defined as lasting or being likely to last for 'a year or more', and 'substantial' is defined as 'more than minor or trivial'. The definition includes sensory impairments such as those affecting sight or hearing, and, just as crucially for schools, children with long-term health conditions such as asthma, diabetes, epilepsy and cancer.

As the SEND Code of Practice (Department for Education, 2014, p. 16) states, the definition for disability provides a relatively low threshold and includes many more children than schools may realise. Children and young people with some conditions do not necessarily have SEN, but there is often a significant overlap between disabled children and young people and those with SEN. Where a disabled child or young person requires special educational provision, they also will be covered by the SEN duties.

The Equality Act applies to all schools, including academies and free schools, university technical colleges and studio schools, and also further education colleges and sixth form colleges – even where the school or college has no disabled pupils currently on roll. This is because the duties under the Equality Act are anticipatory in that they cover not only current pupils but also prospective ones. The expectation is that all schools will be reviewing accessibility continually and making reasonable adjustments in order to improve access for disabled pupils. When thinking about disabled access, the first thing that school leaders usually consider is physical access, such as wheelchair access, lifts and ramps. But physical access is only part of the requirement of the Equality Act and often is the simplest to improve. Your school's accessibility plan for disabled pupils must address all of three elements of planned improvements in access:

1. physical improvements to increase access to education and associated services;
2. improvements in access to the curriculum;
3. improvements in the provision of information for disabled pupils in a range of formats.

Improvements in access to the curriculum are often a harder nut to crack as they involve all departments and all teachers looking closely at their teaching and learning strategies and evaluating how effectively these meet the needs of disabled pupils. Often, relatively minor amendments to the curriculum or teaching approaches can lead to major improvements in access for disabled pupils, and these often have a positive impact on the education of all pupils. For example, one school installed a Soundfield amplification system in a number of classrooms because a pupil with a hearing loss had joined the school. The following year, the cohort of Year 7 pupils had particularly poor speaking and listening skills and it was noticed that they were more engaged in learning when they were taught in the rooms with the Soundfield system. This led to improvements in progress for the whole cohort and significantly reduced the level of disruption and off-task behaviours in those classes.

Schools also have wider duties under the Equality Act to prevent discrimination, to promote equality of opportunity and to foster good relations. These duties should inform all aspects of school improvement planning from curriculum design through to anti-bullying policies and practice.

Significantly, a pupil's underachievement or behaviour difficulties might relate to an underlying physical or mental impairment which could be covered by the Equality Act. Each pupil is different and will respond to situations in his or her unique way, so a disability should be considered in the context of the child as an individual. The 'social model' of disability sees the environment as the primary disabling factor, as opposed to the 'medical model' that focuses on the individual child's needs and difficulties. School activities and environments should be considered in the light of possible barriers to learning or participation.

Appendix 2

Departmental policy

Whether the practice in your school is to have separate SEND policies for each department or to embed the information on SEND in your whole school Inclusion or Teaching and Learning policies, the processes and information detailed below will still be relevant.

Good practice for pupils with SEN and disabilities is good practice for all pupils, especially those who are 'vulnerable' to underachievement. **Vulnerable groups** may include looked-after children (LAC), pupils for whom English is an additional language (EAL), pupils from minority ethnic groups, young carers, and pupils known to be eligible for free school meals/Pupil Premium funding. Be especially aware of those pupils with SEND who face one or more additional vulnerabilities and for whom effective support might need to go beyond help in the classroom.

It is crucial that your departmental or faculty policy describes a strategy for meeting pupils' special educational needs within your particular curricular area. The policy should set the scene for any visitor, from supply staff to inspectors, and make a valuable contribution to the department handbook. The process of developing a departmental SEND policy offers the opportunity to clarify and evaluate current thinking and practice within the faculty and to establish a consistent approach.

The SEND policy for your department is a significant document in terms of the leadership and management of your subject. The preparation and review of the policy should be led by a senior manager within the team because that person needs to have sufficient status to be able to influence subsequent practice and training across the department.

What should a departmental policy contain?

The starting points for your departmental SEND policy will be the whole school SEND policy and the SEND Information Report that, under the Children and

Families Act 2014, all schools are required to publish. Each subject department's own policy should then 'flesh out' the detail in a way that describes how things will work in practice. Writing the policy needs to be much more than a paper exercise completed merely to satisfy the senior management team and Ofsted inspectors. Rather, it is an opportunity for your staff to come together as a team to create a framework for teaching music/performing arts in a way that makes your subject accessible not only to pupils with special educational needs and disabilities, but to all pupils in the school. It is also an ideal opportunity to discuss the impact of grouping on academic and social outcomes for pupils. Bear in mind that the Code of Practice includes a specific duty that 'schools must ensure that pupils with SEND engage in the activities of the school alongside pupils who do not have SEND' (6.2, p. 92).

Who should be involved in developing our SEND policy?

The job of developing and reviewing your policy will be easier if tackled as a joint endeavour. Involve people who will be able to offer support and guidance such as:

- the school SEND governor;
- the SENCO or other school leader with responsibility for SEND;
- your support staff, including teaching assistants and technicians;
- the school data manager, who will be able to offer information about the attainment and progress of different groups;
- outside experts from your local authority, academy chain or other schools;
- parents of pupils with SEND;
- pupils themselves – both with and without SEND.

Bringing together a range of views and information will enable you to develop a policy that is compliant with the letter **and** principle of the legislation, that is relevant to the context of your school, and that is useful in guiding practice and improving outcomes for all pupils.

The role of parents in developing your departmental SEND policy

As outlined in Appendix 1, Section 19 of the Children and Families Act 2014 raises the bar of expectations about how parents should be involved in and influence the work of schools. Not only is it best practice to involve parents of pupils with SEND in the development of policy, but it will also help in 'getting it right' for both pupils and staff. There are a number of ways, both formal and informal, to find out the views of parents to inform policy writing, including:

- focus group;
- coffee morning/drop-in;
- questionnaire/online survey;
- phone survey of a sample of parents.

Parents will often respond more readily if the request for feedback or the invitation to attend a meeting comes from their son or daughter.

Where to start when writing a policy

An audit can act as a starting point for reviewing current policy on SEND or writing a new policy. This will involve gathering information and reviewing current practice with regard to pupils with SEND and is best completed by the whole department, preferably with some input from the SENCO or another member of staff with responsibility for SEND within the school. An audit carried out by the whole department provides a valuable opportunity for professional development so long as it is seen as an exercise in sharing good practice and encourages joint planning. It may also facilitate your department's contribution to the school provision map. But before embarking on an audit, it is worth investing some time in a departmental meeting, or ideally a training day, to raise awareness of the legislation around special educational needs and disabilities and to establish a shared philosophy across your department.

The following headings may be useful when you are establishing your departmental policy:

General statement of compliance

- What is the overarching aim of the policy? What outcomes do you want to achieve for pupils with SEND?
- How are you complying with legislation and guidance?
- What does the school SEND Information Report say about teaching and learning and provision for pupils with SEND?

> **Example**
>
> All members of the department will ensure that the needs of all pupils with SEND are met, according to the aims of the school and its SEND policy . . .

Definition of SEND

- What does SEND mean?
- What are the areas of need and the categories used in the Code of Practice?
- Are there any special implications for our subject area?

(See Chapter 1.)

Provision for staff within the department

- Who has responsibility for SEND within the department?
- What are the responsibilities of this role? E.g.:

  - liaison between the department and the SENCO;
  - monitoring the progress of and outcomes for pupils with SEND, e.g. identifying attainment gaps between pupils with SEND and their peers;
  - attending any liaison meetings and providing feedback to colleagues;
  - attending and contributing to training;
  - maintaining departmental SEND information and records;
  - representing the needs of pupils with SEND at the departmental level;
  - liaising with parents of pupils with SEND;
  - gathering feedback from pupils with SEND on the impact of teaching and support strategies on their learning and well-being.

(This post can be seen as a valuable development opportunity for staff, and the name of this person should be included in the policy. However, where responsibility for SEND is given to a relatively junior member of the team, there must be support and supervision from the head of the department to ensure that the needs of pupils with SEND have sufficient prominence in both policy and practice.)

- What information about pupils' SEND is held? Where is it stored and how is it shared?
- How can staff access additional resources, information and training?
- How will staff ensure effective planning and communication between teachers and teaching assistants?
- What assessments are available for teachers in your department to support accurate identification of SEND?

> **Example**
>
> The member of staff with responsibility for overseeing the provision of SEND within the department will attend liaison meetings and subsequently give feedback to the other members of the department. S/he will maintain the department's SEND file, attend and/or organise appropriate training and disseminate this to all departmental staff. All information will be treated with confidentiality.

Provision for pupils with SEND

- How are pupils' special educational needs identified? E.g.:

  - observation in lessons;
  - assessment of class work/homework;
  - end of module tests/progress checks;
  - annual examinations/SATs/GCSEs;
  - reports.

- How is progress measured for pupils with SEND?
- How do members of the department contribute to individual learning plans, meetings with parents and reviews?
- What criteria are used for organising teaching groups?
- How/when can pupils move between groups?
- What adjustments are made for pupils with special educational needs and/ or disabilities in lessons and homework?
- How do we use information about pupils' abilities in reading, writing, speaking and listening when planning lessons and homework?
- What alternative courses are available for pupils with SEND?
- What special arrangements are made for internal and external examinations?
- What guidance is available for working effectively with support staff?

Here is a good place also to put a statement about the school behaviour policy and any rewards and sanctions, and how the department will make any necessary adjustments to meet the needs of pupils with SEND.

> **Example**
>
> The staff in the [subject] department will aim to support pupils with SEND to achieve the best possible outcomes. They will do this by supporting pupils to achieve their individual targets as specified in their individual

learning plans, and will provide feedback for progress reviews. Pupils with SEND will be included in the departmental monitoring system used for all pupils.

Resources and learning materials

- Is any specialist equipment used in the department?
- How are differentiated resources developed? What criteria do we use (e.g. literacy levels)?
- Where are resources stored and are they accessible for both staff and pupils?

Example

The department will provide suitably differentiated materials and, where appropriate, specialist instruments/resources to meet the needs of pupils with SEND. Alternative courses and examinations will be made available where appropriate for individual pupils. Support staff will be provided with curriculum information in advance of lessons and will be involved in lesson planning. A list of resources is available in the department handbook.

Staff qualifications and continuing professional development (CPD)

- What qualifications and experience do the members of the department have?
- What training has already taken place, and when? What impact did that training have on teaching and learning, and progress for pupils with SEND?
- How is training planned? What criteria are used to identify training needs?
- What account of SEND is taken when new training opportunities are proposed?
- Is a record kept of training completed and ongoing training needs?

Example

A record of training undertaken, specialist skills and training required will be kept in the department handbook. Requests for training will be considered in line with the department and school improvement plan.

Monitoring and reviewing the policy

- How will the policy be monitored?
- Who will lead the monitoring?
- When will the policy be reviewed?

Example

The departmental SEND policy will be monitored by the head of department on a planned annual basis, with advice being sought from the SENCO as part of the three-yearly review process.

Conclusion

Creating a departmental SEND policy should be a developmental activity that will improve teaching and learning for all pupils, but especially for those who are vulnerable to underachievement. The policy should be a working document that will evolve and change over time; it is there to challenge current practice and to encourage improvement for both pupils and staff. If departmental staff work together to create the policy, they will have ownership of it; it will have true meaning and be effective in clarifying good practice.

An example of a departmental policy for you to amend is available on the website: www.routledge.com/9781138231849.

Appendix 3

Case studies

1. Jed, Year 9 (autistic spectrum disorder)
2. Janine, Year 7 (hearing impairment)
3. Dale, Year 10 (moderate learning difficulties)
4. Julia, Year 9 (visual impairment)
5. Natasha, Year 8 (dyslexia)
6. David, Year 10 (social, emotional and mental health difficulties)

1 Jed, Year 9 (autistic spectrum disorder)

Jed is in Year 9 and is autistic. When he first came to the music lessons in the high school, Jed would run out of the room when anyone played a loud sound or put his hands over his ears and scream. The teacher thought this was because the sounds were frightening him or that he had really sensitive hearing. After a term the teacher and the TA began to realise that he was fine in the lessons provided he was prepared for the sounds of some of the instruments such as the drum kit and the trumpet. If this was done, he would actually enjoy listening to them.

In order to help him, the TA started to use a PECS book (Picture Exchange Communication System): this has Velcro lines on each page, to which picture cards can be attached. The TA uses this to set out a timetable for Jed each day – some of the pictures are of an object of reference for the subject, some are a picture of the teacher. This is especially useful for preparing Jed for anything that is going to be different from the normal routine.

In music lessons, the TA has a supply of pictures of the instruments (made by using the school's digital camera) and shows these to Jed before they are played. He is now able to understand what will happen next and can remain calm. Jed is also able to point to the picture of the instrument he would like to play and exchange the picture for the instrument.

By the end of Year 8 Jed would not just tolerate the loudest of the instruments, but actually seemed to enjoy them.

Much of the time Jed didn't appear to be paying any attention in lessons, but the TA would sometimes catch him singing part of a song they had learned three or four weeks before. She started to keep a diary of these occurrences and realised that he had in fact been taking in much of the lesson content.

If the lesson was based around rhythm notation, Jed could always clap the rhythm straight away, and if he listened to a melody on the keyboard, he was able to repeat it without any mistakes, often after only one hearing. The teacher and TA were only able to discover this when they had put in strategies to calm him down; thus it took a long time to understand the extent of his abilities. He could still be disturbed or not concentrating during the lessons, but by now the staff were more confident in finding ways to help him.

The teacher is now considering entering Jed for GCSE Music and has designed a programme for him which works well alongside all the other pupils in the class. This consists of rhythm work using notation, playing basic tunes on the keyboard for him to copy, playing chords on chime bars, and then transferring these to the keyboard using Foxwood Song Sheets. Jed has directed a group of pupils when to play and when to stop.

2 Janine, Year 7 (hearing impairment)

Janine is in Year 7 and has a cochlear implant. She communicates using a mixture of speech and sign language.

She enjoys music lessons and is hoping to be able to learn the cello with a peripatetic teacher who visits the school.

The music teacher has always encouraged Janine to join in the music lessons. This has resulted in her doing a lot of basic percussion sessions which have enabled her to develop her good sense of rhythm. She particularly enjoyed playing the bass drum and the congas.

During a recent school production she was chosen to play the xylophone. She found it quite easy to learn how to play the piece by watching the teacher demonstrate it and to understand where the pattern of notes was the same and where it changed. The teacher had been teaching form and had explained that the piece had the form ABAA; this understanding made it easier for Janine to play. She found that she needed to remember the piece because she needed to watch her hands as she played to make sure she had the correct notes – as she was not able to hear them all clearly (especially when the others were playing). Playing next to her friend helped. Although she learned the notes quickly, she found it hard when she had to maintain a steady pulse and to play the long notes the right length. She realised that she found the music easy to play when there was a note on every beat, but struggled with the longer notes, finding it hard to imagine the length of time needed for the minims and semibreves.

The music teacher suggested that Janine should try some country dancing. This was not easy; walking and dancing in time with all the other people proved very difficult and required a lot of concentration. However, by the end of the term she found she understood how to play better because of the dancing. The constant counting of eight and four beats had fixed the patterns in her mind, and she was able to imagine the length of the long notes and understand the pattern of the four phrases ABAA better.

3 Dale, Year 10 (moderate learning difficulties)

Dale is working towards the Welsh Board Entry Level certificate.

The class are writing a song, concentrating on how to give the melody structure chords. They have listened as a group to a variety of songs from different cultures and have noted the form of these.

Many pupils in the class have already written several songs. The music teacher has written down a set of activities for the TA to work through with Dale over the next four weeks which will lead to him creating his own 16 bar piece:

1. Play the notes of the pentatonic to get used to the sound. He uses a xylophone with the pentatonic scale CDEGA. The TA encourages him to play the notes for a while, letting him listen to the sounds. He doesn't do this for long.
2. Think of a subject and create a short poem. The TA suggests that he tries to think of some words which he would like to use. He finds this easy and lists his favourite friends. He is able to use this idea to say several lines which the TA writes down as a four line stanza.
3. Clap the rhythm of the words you've written; together the TA and Dale clap this many times. Dale does not find this easy. The TA gets a drum and he enjoys this more, although it is quite difficult. They try claves – he finds this easier and starts to be able to play the pattern.
4. Using the notes of the pentatonic, create your first line A. Dale plays on the instrument again, finding a pattern that he likes. The TA writes this down as melody using letter names. They record the sounds as he goes along onto a tape recorder.

5. Find a different set of notes for line B. Dale experiments and then settles on a group of notes he likes. He notes it down as B, writing down the letter names. They record it.

6. Put your ideas together in the form AABA. They use the two tunes Dale has written in the pattern given. Dale is not sure about using the same tune three times, but the teacher reassures him that they sing many songs which do this, finding an example for him to listen to.

7. Either sing your tune yourself or ask a friend to do it for you onto the tape. Dale wants to sing the song. He has been listening to the tape of the song at home and is really happy to perform it through a microphone for the rest of the class. The teacher plays the tune. They record it.

8. Add chords to this. This is too difficult for Dale, but he is happy to hear his tune played with the chords added by the teacher. She marks these in for him in large letters, and then asks two other pupils to come and accompany Dale on the guitar and drums. The teacher is able to record this as a piece which Dale has composed (noting the part played by herself and the TA) and can also use this as an ensemble performance.

4 Julia, Year 9 (visual impairment)

Julia has private lessons at home on the piano and on the flute. Although she loves her school, she finds the music lessons quite difficult.

The teacher has asked the class to write a song, working with partners. Julia is sharing a keyboard with her best friend, Alice. They each have headphones so that they can work together on the piece; Julia finds them difficult and uncomfortable, but if she takes them off she can't concentrate because of all the other noises in the classroom.

Her friend is writing down the tune, and Julia is recording any good musical ideas on her own personal mini-disk recorder.

They are both trying to think of words for the piece.

Eventually, Julia decides she will finish the tune at home and asks Alice to do the words.

In the next lesson, the teacher realises that Julia is finding it difficult to work with the headphones on and allows Julia and Alice to work in a practice room. They then get on really quickly and produce a really good song which Alice is going to sing, with Julia playing the accompaniment.

They perform it in the summer concert.

They spend two music lessons practising the piece on the concert stage, and Alice helps the TA put chairs and music stands out as if the orchestra and the other players are there. As a result, on the concert night Julia is able to move reasonably confidently to her playing position only minimally guided by Alice.

In order to create a really good ensemble and avoid counting aloud to start, Julia has added an introduction. She starts the piece when the concert hall is really quiet, with Alice joining in at the appropriate time.

5 Natasha, Year 8 (dyslexia)

Natasha finds that she is very good at music and enjoys playing the piano by ear and singing almost every advert on the television. However, since coming into Year 8, she has begun to dread her music lessons.

At the beginning of the term the new teacher informed the class that she wanted them all to be able to read music by the end of the year. In fact, many of the pupils have private lessons and have been reading music for many years. Natasha doesn't tell her friends how much she enjoys playing the piano in case they ask her to sight-read a new tune. She is very worried about the new teacher's plan and starts to sit at the back of the classroom and sometimes gets into trouble for messing about.

The teacher has realised that although there are many in the class who read music easily, there are some for whom it is going to be really difficult. She is aware that Natasha is dyslexic but is not sure how this will affect her music making.

In order to put all the class on a level playing field she decides to teach them all to read tonic sol fah using the Kodály method which she had learned on a Voices Foundation Course. This system uses hand signs to indicate relative pitch. There is a sign for each note of the major scale.

Natasha cannot believe it when she finds that she does not have to look at small dots on lines. (In the past when she had tried this, they often appeared to move about, and she found it very difficult to follow a line all the way across the page – she heard that this was called a 'mid line flick'.) She also finds that because she has spent a lot of time listening to the notes and playing by ear, she is very good at this method of 'reading music'. She decides that she would like to sit at the front of the class now.

By the end of the year she can read a whole song from the signs. The teacher has fulfilled her aim as all the rest of the class have discovered this different way of reading music.

6 David, Year 10 (social, emotional and mental health difficulties)

David has an education, health and care plan because of his behavioural difficulties. He also has very poor handwriting skills and, having been excluded from school several times, he has missed whole chunks of his education. He is embarrassed about his writing and tries to do as little as possible. He has his own drum kit at home and plays for the local youth club rock band.

Although he loves playing drum kit, he hates all other musical activities and habitually engages in low level violence against other pupils. He also upsets the other pupils with inappropriate remarks about sex. He is frequently in the referral/inclusion room where he is sent for infringing the classroom rules.

Playing drum kit is the one place where David is better than most other pupils. His self-esteem demonstrably rises when he is performing in class, to the school or just to the peripatetic drum kit teacher, with whom he has a good relationship. He loves other people knowing how good he is and frequently asks if he is better than Catriona, the school's other top drummer (they are roughly the same standard).

When he is playing drum kit at concerts outside school, he always tries his best. Sometimes at rehearsals he sulks and ruins it for the school's jazz/rock band. Then he may choose not to come to rehearsals for weeks on end.

The music teacher and the SENCO have negotiated with the head of year that, whatever David has done, his peripatetic lesson is an entitlement that he should never miss. Whenever his language or behaviour becomes unacceptable, the music teacher confines herself to a brief 'Less of the bad language, David', and goes on to praise somebody else's work, making sure that David hears her do it.

David is unlikely to get a good grade for GCSE as he has no interest in the listening and composing elements of the exam. But the music teacher thinks she may motivate him by broadening his experience of other live music. He could not sit still or keep quiet when she took the class to the local operatic society's version of *Carmen*, but the teacher had anticipated this and had a school mentor with her who took David home early. (The mentor told David that she couldn't stay till the end, and would he like a lift early as she lived near.)

Next day he talked a lot about the opera, which was quite outside his normal experience. The music teacher continues to look for other musical events, such as local carnivals and 'battles of the bands', where he can broaden his listening experience and participate as a member of the audience and not as the 'star'. He is taking the Rock School drum kit exams with the peripatetic drum teacher, who is also trying to develop other percussion skills (e.g. timbale and congas). The teacher gets him to work with Catriona in a friendly and competitive way and has negotiated with other subject teachers that sometimes he may 'cool off' in the music room. For David, music and drumming constitute a personal lifeline.

Appendix 4

Guidelines for effective teaching in music lessons

Students on equal terms	Music can be something that pupils with additional needs can do on equal terms with everyone else. Don't underestimate musical ability or be surprised by perfect pitch. Sometimes playing an idea will be quicker than explaining it. It may be better to use music as the main means of communication rather than speaking.
Barriers to learning	Avoid depending too much on spoken language when teaching. Information such as a history of the instruments may not be understood and means less time for music playing. Too much talk may lead to disruptive behaviour or 'switching off': keep instructions short and clear and be prepared to repeat if necessary.
Clear instructions	Use modelling, simple signs or pictures. Simplify instructions – this may mean more words not fewer. Use a visual timetable to show how the lesson will run.
Pace and patience	Do give time for an idea or instruction to sink in. Have short focused activities. Have a plan with lots of ways of practising the same skill – but be willing to follow the pupil if they become engaged with an activity.
Routines	Develop useful routines, repeating the structure and the activity in the same way until well established. Progress will only be made with practice.
Praise	Praise carefully, accurately and for small identifiable steps. Develop a repertoire of graded comments to suit the actual achievement made. Avoid overpraising.
Ignore tactically	Ignore any behaviour which doesn't impede the flow of the lesson or stop others learning.
Positive and negative	Use positive language: 'This is how I would like you to do this'. Avoid: 'Don't do it like that'.

Appendix 5

Individual behaviour plan

Pupil *A Somebody* **Form** *9JP*	**DOB** *11/1/2003*
IBP NO *10* **Start Date** *9/9/06*	**Review Date** *11/11/16*

Concerns

Poor behaviour

Details

- *Arrives late for lessons*
- *Disruptive behaviour in class*
- *Reluctant to follow instructions*
- *Does very little work in class*

Targets to be achieved	Achieved		
in music lessons	**Yes**		**No**
1 *Arrives on time for lessons*			
2 *Completes the tasks set*			
3 *Allows other pupils to get on with their work*			

Strategies

- *Regular home contact*
- *In class support*
- *Praise for good behaviour*
- *Encourage to attend the drummers club on Thursdays*

Staff **Key Worker** *A Person* **LS Co-ordinator** *A A Person*	

Monitoring and assessment

- *Daily target cards*
- *Half term reviews*

Individual behaviour plan

Pupil Form	DOB
IBP NO **Start Date**	**Review Date**

Concerns

Details

Targets to be achieved	Achieved		
	Yes		**No**
1			
2			
3			
4			
5			

Strategies

Staff **Key Worker** **LS Co-ordinator**	

Monitoring and assessment

References

All website URLs below were accessed on 16 December 2016.

Websites

Accessible Arts and Media: York-based charity that champions and celebrates the skills and talents of local communities, young people and adults with disabilities, www.aamedia.org.uk

Apollo Creative: Accessible switch technology suitable for playing and composing, www.apollocreative.co.uk

AQA unit award scheme: UAS – unit award scheme – based on a record of achievement, www.aqa.org.uk/programmes/unit-award-scheme/organisations-that-use-uas/sen

Arts Award: Arts Awards encourage young people to explore the arts – they are awards at five different levels, www.artsaward.org.uk

ASDAN: Offers a curriculum in expressive arts with assessment modules suitable for pupils with learning difficulties, www.asdan.org.uk

British Association for Music Therapy (BAMT): The professional body for music therapy in the UK, providing both practitioners and non-practitioners with information, professional support and training opportunities, www.bamt.org

Dalcroze Society: Promotes the use of movement to teach music to children with SEND, http://dalcroze.org.uk

Drake Music: Music technology to support pupils with SEND, www.drakemusic.org

Imuse: Research led technology, making music more accessible to pupils with PMLD, www.aamedia.org.uk/index.php/what-we-do/sensory-programme-for-adults/8-sensory-programme/44-imuse

Inclusive Technology: Supplies switches and technical solutions to access issues, www.inclusive.co.uk

ISM (Incorporated Society of Musicians): Produces online resources for the classroom music teacher, www.ism.org/education

British Kodály Academy (BKA): Promotes a method of music teaching for pupils with SEND, www.britishkodalyacademy.org

LMS supplies: Vibro tactile instruments, http://lmsmusicsupplies.co.uk

Music and the Deaf: Workshops, after school clubs and advice, www.matd.org.uk

Music Mark: Professional teaching organisation which produces online resources for the classroom music teacher, www.musicmark.org.uk

National Curriculum: www.gov.uk/government/collections/national-curriculum

Ocarina: Training for teachers and pupils using their own graphic notation, www.ocarina.co.uk

Orff: Promotes the Orff approach to teaching music, www.orff.org.uk

Sing Up: An online song resource which includes accessible formats, www.singup.org

Soundabout: Regional and national organisation promoting music for children with PMLD and autism; disseminates the Sounds of Intent framework; hosts accredited PGCert in Music and Special Needs, www.soundabout.org.uk

Soundbeam: Multi-sensory equipment and training on its use, www.soundbeam.co.uk

Sounds of Intent framework: An assessment framework for pupils with PMLD, autism and learning difficulties, http://soundsofintent.org

Voices Foundation: Courses on the Kodály method and singing class techniques, www.voices.org.uk

YAMSEN: SpeciallyMusic: Yorkshire Association for Music and SEN, www. yamsen.org.uk

Publications are available (e.g. Foxwood Song Sheets) through Lindsay Music, www.lindsaymusic.co.uk

Books and documents

Corke, M. (2002) *Approaches to Communication through Music*, London: David Fulton.

Department for Education (2014) SEND Code of Practice, www.gov.uk/government/ uploads/system/uploads/attachment_data/file/398815/SEND_Code_of_Practice_ January_2015.pdf.

Miles, T.R. and Westcombe, J. (2001) *Music and Dyslexia*, London: Whurr.

Nind, M. and Hewett, D. (2006) *Interaction in Action*, 2nd edn. London: David Fulton, www.intensiveinteraction.co.uk.

Ockleford, A. (2013) *Music, Language and Autism: Exceptional Strategies for Exceptional Minds*, London: Jessica Kingsley.

Prevezer, W. (2002) *Entering into Interaction*, 3rd edn. Available from the Elizabeth Newson Centre, 272 Longdale Lane, Ravenshead, Nottingham, NG15 9AH.

Zimmerman, S. (1998) *Instrumental Music*, London: RNIB.

National organisations for SEND

Action on Hearing Loss, 020 7296 8000, www.actiononhearingloss.org.uk

Autism Education Trust, 020 7903 3650, www.autismeducationtrust.org.uk

British Dyslexia Association (BDA) gives advice on issues related to music making for dyslexic pupils, www.bdadyslexia.org.uk

Down's Syndrome Association, 0333 1212 300, www.downs-syndrome.org.uk

Dyspraxia Foundation, 01462 455 016, www.dyspraxiafoundation.org.uk

Foundation for People with Learning Disabilities, 020 7803 1100, www. learningdisabilities.org.uk

Mencap, 020 7454 0454, www.mencap.org.uk

National Association for Special Educational Needs (NASEN), www.nasen.org.uk

National Autistic Society, 020 7833 2299, www.autism.org.uk

National Deaf Children's Society (general advice, plus resources and advice for supporting music making with deaf pupils), 020 7490 8656, www.ndcs.org.uk

Royal National Institute of Blind People (RNIB), 030 3123 9999, www.rnib.org.uk

Scope, 0808 800 3333, www.scope.org.uk

SEBDA, 01233 622958, www.sebda.org

Tourettes Action UK, 0300 777 8427 (Helpdesk), www.tourettes-action.org.uk

Index